Launching New Products

Launching New Products

Best Marketing and Sales Practices

John Westman and Paul Sowyrda

BUSINESS EXPERT PRESS

Launching New Products: Best Marketing and Sales Practices

First published in 2016 by
Business Expert Press, LLC
222 East 46th Street, New York, NY 10017
www.businessexpertpress.com

ISBN-13: 978-1-60649-922-1 (paperback)
ISBN-13: 978-1-60649-923-8 (e-book)

Business Expert Press Marketing Strategy Collection

Collection ISSN: 2150-9654 (print)
Collection ISSN: 2150-9662 (electronic)

Cover and interior design by Exeter Premedia Services Private Ltd., Chennai, India

First edition: 2016

10 9 8 7 6 5 4 3 2 1

Printed in the United States of America.

I would like to thank the many people who have taught, inspired, and guided me on the path that led to this book, including Paul Sowryda, Philip Kotler, Jeanne Brett, Tom Kuczmarski, Margaret Maurer, James Nichols, Tom Ritchie, Bill Burns, Arthur Holden, Gail Gaumer, Larry Rohrer, Matt Pearman, Brent Wentz, Sharon George, Skip Ashmore, Joe Walsh, Rob Kanzer, Mike Schrader, Pete Newcomb, Barbara Reeder, Lionel Bihm, Chris Kontzen, Loretta Keane, Joan L'Esperance, Daniel Pascheles, Luc De Langhe, Rob Zwettler, Gerald Smith, Vicki Crittenden, Jonathan Lorch, Martin Schreiber, Karl Nolph, Dimitri Oreopoulus, Emil Paganini, Jack Falvey, Jim Freedman, Peter Sauer, Bob Grant, Ames and Joan Abbot, Michelle and Tim Techler and family, Alison Brown and family, Louis Gudema, Dan Hawkins, Rob Kanzer, Doug McGuire, Mark DiOrio, Peg Flanagan, Murray Decock, Gene Kennedy, Brian Schiff, Tom Collishaw, Marianne Crosley, Jeremy Gould, Marie-Joelle Pradayrol, Ron and Sue Tracy, Patrick and Barbara and Emma Clear, John Krohn, Paul Kollberg, John Murphy, Doug Dittmann, John Ritchie, Frank Remington, Mike Koval, Troy and Nicole and Matthew and Tyler Randall, Margot Rendall, George Gardner, Sue Mazingo, Linda Branch, Kathleen Grant, Amber Bobin, Jennifer Schiffmacher, Paul and Tatiana and Anaise and Tresor Rusesabagina, and Carine Kanimba, Jan and Matthew and Carly and Luke Westman, Dan and Alison and Peter and Eric and Alex Westman, Eric and Gretchen and Laura and Megan and Clay Westman, Jack and Nancy Westman, John and Jean Hummon, Marcus and Levi and Caney and Moses Hummon and Becca Stevens, Sarah and Brian and Tess and Anna and Griffin Stevens, Gretchen Hummon and Peter and Trevor and Phoebe and Malcolm Fry, students from my Boston College and Harvard Extension courses, and many Thistle Farmers.

I am grateful to John Westman, John Sowyrda Jr., Bernard Wasserman, Dick Falb and James Melsa for being key mentors, coaches, friends and important people in my life.

Abstract

The goals of this book are (1) to share best practices of launching new products with professionals who want to help customers and make their company successful, and (2) to stimulate more conversations about how to successfully launch new products. The practices in this book were derived from hundreds of publications and over 60 years of experience launching over 50 new products. These practices represent the experience of its authors, and hopefully will cause other effective practices to be documented and shared.

So, why this book? New product launches can be more effective! What is the ultimate measure of effectiveness? Sales dollars, profit dollars, and growth rates are excellent measures. But how do you know that the launch is the best it can be? There is no endorsed standard that is used to evaluate the actions leading up to the launch, and corrective actions used during the product launch. As a result, business leaders make their own judgments and never truly know how much more successful they could have been.

Why isn't there an objective standard? There is none, and will likely never be, and there are no well-designed studies that prove the effectiveness of new product launches. Each product launch has a unique market, company, and product dynamics. Unfortunately, the people leading product launches do not use fundamental marketing approaches because either they are not aware of them or they do not believe in them. Product launch decisions are even based on the biases of company leaders who may have limited experience, or unsuccessful experience, in launching new products. These people simply have no understanding of what they are doing and are even unaware of what they are missing.

Airline pilots and surgeons have checklists because the consequence of missing a task can be catastrophic. Checklists for pilots and surgeons save lives.

The goals of this book are to discuss critical topics in launching new products, and to distill successful approaches from hundreds of publications and experience from launching over 50 new products into a checklist for marketing leaders, CEOs, and board members. The function of this checklist is to force consideration and completion of tasks that drive a successful product launch.

Our hypothesis is that companies will increase their probability of a successful new product launch by using this checklist. This checklist will ensure that you have covered the fundamentals, and it will save you time researching proven practices. This checklist highlights important factors that create a successful product launch and is structured to follow the Marketing's 4P's—product, price, promotion, and place (distribution) (citation). The new product launch checklist is shown in Appendix 1.

In addition to a checklist, the organization needs an experienced *pilot* or leader who can select and prioritize initiatives, delete irrelevant items, and add new items specific to the unique product launch. By using this checklist, the new product launch leader can be confident that he or she has considered critical tasks and, therefore, will improve the probability of maximizing the value of the product launch to customers and company stakeholders.

So, use this checklist, hire an experienced pilot and maximize your new product launch!

Keywords

Best practices, checklist, marketing, new products, new product introduction, new product launch, professional selling

Contents

Introduction xi

Chapter 1   Context of the New Product Launch 1
Chapter 2   New Product Launch Team Leadership Approach 23
Chapter 3   Marketing Mix: The 4 P's 33
Chapter 4   Messaging, Professional Selling, Raving Fans, and
             Customer Development 55
Chapter 5   Sales Training, Value Propositions, the Brand Promise,
             Pricing, Legal, and Ethical Considerations 85
Chapter 6   New Product Launch Checklist 119

Appendixes 127
References 135
Index 137

Introduction

Outstanding marketers have many titles and come from diverse backgrounds. The best marketers are exceptional learners. They are curious, systematic, adaptive, urgent, inspirational, mostly joyful, and love measuring results of activities.

Unfortunately, there are also many marketers who are pretenders. The pretenders will tell you that they *know* what to do rather than sharing their plan. The pretenders won't create a system to get customer feedback and measure activities. The pretenders reduce the success of new product launches. They also tarnish the reputation of the marketing discipline because while they call their work marketing, their work lacks the rigor and success rate of thoughtful, professional marketing. The pretenders have many titles and diverse backgrounds. They tend to tell rather than ask, tend to lack rigorous training and experience in marketing fundamentals, are unrealistic, and create dysfunctional rather than winning teams. This checklist can be a performance enhancement tool for outstanding marketers and an inoculation or insurance against pretenders.

Airline pilots have a preflight checklist. Surgeons have a preoperation checklist. These checklists must be completed prior to each flight or surgery because the consequences of missing a preparation step could be catastrophic. Companies need a product launch checklist. This checklist must be completed prior to each product launch because the consequence of missing an essential preparation step will reduce the success of the product and the value it brings to customers and the company.

"... we need a different strategy for overcoming failures, one that builds on experience and takes advantage of the knowledge people have but somehow also makes up for our inevitable human inadequacies. And there is such a strategy .... It is a checklist." (Gawande 2010, 13)

The new product launch checklist will improve the commercial success of new products and services. However, please keep in mind that certain tasks in the checklist will not be relevant to your situation, some will need modification, and some situations will need additional tasks.

We will consider this book a success when it is used to create productive conversations on important tasks required for maximizing the success of your specific product launch.

The target audience for this book is business leaders who want to capture maximum value from introducing a new product or service. Each product introduction occurs in a unique moment in time, in a market with unique characteristics, and in competitive circumstances by a unique company with individuals performing tasks for the launch. Even with these varied circumstances, this checklist will increase the success of the new product and company because it focuses on fundamental tasks.

CHAPTER 1

Context of the New Product Launch

Marketing will be the basic motivating force for the entire corporation. Soon it will be true that every activity of the corporation – from finance to sales to production – is aimed at satisfying the needs and desires of the consumer. When that stage of development is reached, the marketing revolution will be complete.

—Robert Keith, 1960.

Marketing's ultimate role in the firm is to drive creation of value for buyers and capture ... a significant part of that created value for the company.

—John Farley.

Context of the New Product Launch—the CEO's World and How Marketing Helps

New product launches occur in the broader context of the relationship of the CEO and the marketing effort. The CEO is often juggling diverse company activities such as managing the board, raising money, communicating with investors, and leading the company strategy (see Figure 1.1). Due to the CEO's complicated function, the CEO needs the help of the marketing leader to create a systematic, thoughtful plan that will give the organization the best chance at sustained competitive advantage, success in the market, and financial success.

The relationship between the CEO, the marketing leader, and team and creating value for the company are depicted in the Marketing Pyramid™ (Figure __). As shown in this diagram, the overriding goal of the CEO is to increase the valuation of the company. The CEO's

Figure 1.1 CEO's worldview

internally focused function is to increase the company's value. The CEO can do this most effectively by ensuring that the company is focused on its target customer needs and that all functions in the company are aligned so that target customers prefer working with the company and help the company evolve to satisfy even more of their needs. The CEO works with the marketing leader to ensure the marketing and sales plan is clear, executed, and measured for continual improvement.

The marketing function was created by the CEO to amplify the CEO's ability to understand and satisfy the target customer needs, as well as improve the alignment and integration of the company so it can get, keep, and grow profitable customers.

The Marketing Pyramid (Figure 1.2) depicts the relationship of the marketing department with the CEO and the breadth of functions of an effective marketing department. The relationship between the successful marketing leader and the CEO is characterized by powerful conversations (citation), or conversations that contain two of the three following elements:

- Enhance the relationship between the marketing leader and CEO;
- Contain an *ah-ha* or significant learning moment; and
- End with an effective action plan.

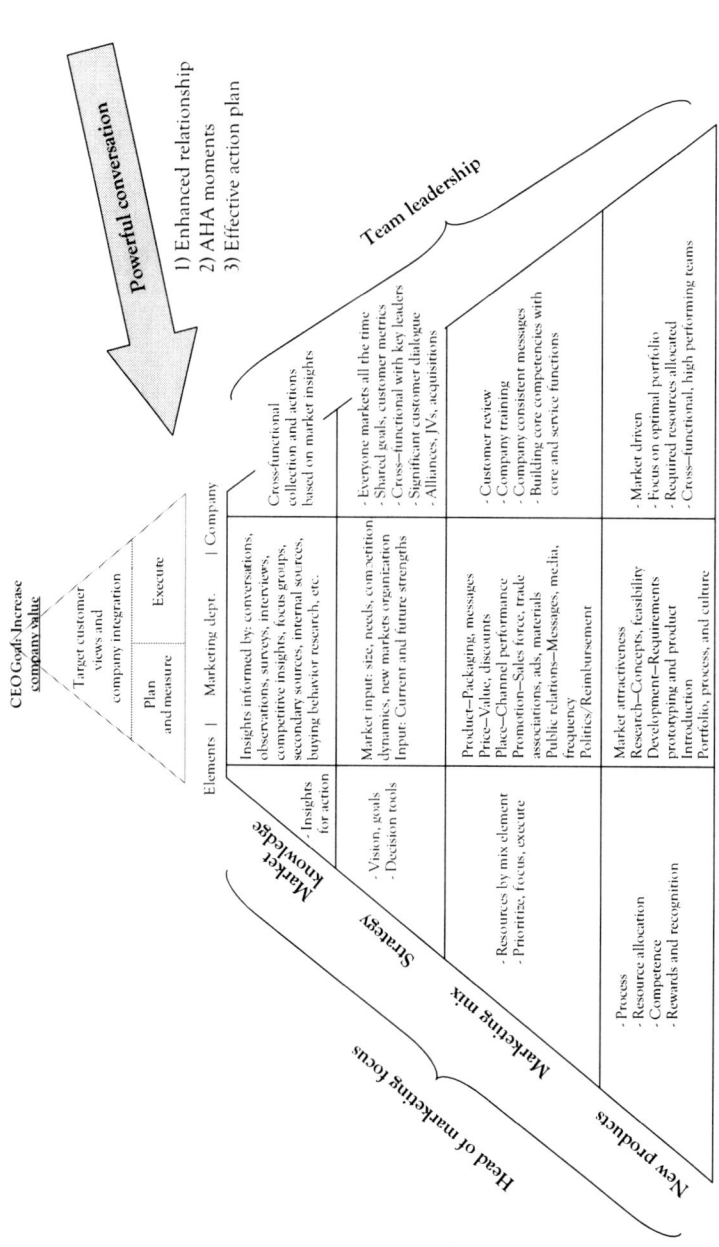

Figure 1.2 Context for CEO, marketing and new product launch

The CEO needs to work with the marketing leader to ensure that the target customer's needs are understood, that the company strategy will create and sustain competitive advantages profitably, and that company functions are integrated and working together effectively. In addition, the CEO must endorse the marketing plan and ensure that the company measures and executes the plan.

The marketing team needs to work with prospects, customers, and colleagues in other functions to create and deliver market knowledge, marketing strategy including competitive intelligence and the marketing mix, and products and services that provide sustainable competitive advantage. In addition to these functions, the marketing team must be experts in team leadership in order to engage prospects, customers, and colleagues in this process.

Market knowledge goes beyond background information and needs to distill insights that can help the company compete. These insights come from the following:

- Conversations with customers and colleagues who are well informed on changes in the market and changes with competitors;
- Observations of customers and competitive activity;
- Product effectiveness studies; and
- Publications or relevant outlets such as social media and conferences.

Market intelligence includes the size of the market in units, sales dollars, and profit dollars; the dominant unmet market needs; competition—today and in the future, dynamics of the government or industry that may cause changes in market size and competitive advantages—potential new markets; and the strengths and weaknesses of the organizations.

The marketing team creates and implements the *marketing mix* that allocates resources and plans projects that impact the product (e.g., product quality, variety, design, features, brand names, packaging, and sizes), price (pricing strategy—value, penetration or competitive, list price, volume discounts, etc.), promotion (e.g., segmentation and targeting, sales force composition and management including materials, and advertising), and place or distribution (e.g., channels, coverage, and offerings per channel).

The marketing team leads the efforts to understand unmet market needs, develops products to meet those needs, and plans and implements the plans that bring the new product to the market and cause the new product to succeed. The majority of this book discusses the activities required to bring a new product to market and create early success.

High-Performance Work Teams

High-performance work teams (HPWT) are created by team leaders who are students and teachers of winning teams. Team leadership is a core competency that the marketing professional needs to bring to each of his or her projects and to help the organization upgrade its team leadership effectiveness. The marketing professional needs to lead by example. A useful tool is the "Ten Characteristics of a High-Performance Work Team," described in the following text.

Overview

Teams offer many potential benefits including increased involvement, development, and empowerment of employees; more effective use of a diverse array of employee skills and capabilities; improved problem solving and decision making; increased creativity; and improved work processes and performance. However, many teams have failed to achieve these successes. This can occur for a variety of reasons, but the most significant reason is the failure to develop the conditions necessary for the creation of an HPWT.

An HPWT is a group (two or more) of interdependent individuals who work together in a specific manner to achieve a common objective. As its name indicates, what separates an HPWT from any other team is its ability to perform at the highest level for an extended period of time and to accomplish its work in the most efficient and effective manner possible. Although purposes, objectives, and roles can change from one team to the next, HPWTs do the following on a consistent basis.

Ten Characteristics of an HPWT

1. *Develop goals and plans.* An HPWT begins with a clearly defined mission that describes the specific purpose for the team's existence. In addition, the team sets goals on a regular basis and is effective at developing and implementing plans. The team members are clear about goals and priorities and consistently act in ways that support the team's overall mission and goals.

2. *Enhance communication among members.* An HPWT has members who freely share information, are open and honest with each other, listen to each other, and provide each other with both positive and constructive feedback. The team also employs a specific process to facilitate the dissemination of information on a regular basis (e.g., informational meetings).

3. *Develop and maintain positive relationships among members.* An HPWT has members who respect, support, cooperate with, and trust each other. Such teams proactively work to build positive relationships by providing opportunities for social interaction, giving assignments that put staff into contact with individuals they don't normally interact *with, and providing cross-training opportunities.*

4. *Solve problems and make decisions on a timely basis.* An HPWT is effective at identifying and resolving problems, as well as making successful group decisions. In addition, the team involves all members in the problem-solving and decision-making processes.

5. *Successfully manage conflict.* An HPWT is effective at identifying and resolving conflicts in a timely and mutually beneficial manner. High-performing teams also minimize the occurrence of conflict by implementing communication and conflict resolution training, incorporating ongoing team-building activities, and encouraging the active participation of all team members.

6. *Facilitate productive meetings.* An HPWT has effective, productive, well-managed meetings that efficiently use team members' time. Every meeting is focused, timely, and necessary and is used to solve problems, make decisions, disseminate information, and enhance the skills of team member.

7. *Clarify roles for team members.* An HPWT has members who know their responsibility and authority, understand the roles that

are played by others, and use everyone's skills and abilities. Team members are also clear about the connection between team goals and their day-to-day activities.

8. *Operate in a productive manner.* An HPWT has the resources and skills needed for success, is able to complete its work in a timely manner, and utilizes quality and productivity measures to evaluate overall *efficiency* (how well team processes are operating) and *effectiveness* (the quality of the team's products and services).

9. *Exhibit effective team leadership.* An HPWT has leaders who define team goals and priorities, facilitate collaboration among team members, manage team performance, and generate opportunities for success. Successful team leaders encourage active participation, clarify priorities on a continuous basis, and work to create a supportive team environment.

10. *Provide development opportunities for team members.* An HPWT provides ongoing development opportunities for team members in technical, interpersonal, and team-building areas. This includes the application of a variety of developmental interventions such as classroom training, coaching and mentoring, development assignments, feedback-based activities, and self-directed learning (Holmes 2012).

Marketing "4Ps" Fundamental Diagnostic Tool

Introduction

How do you benchmark your marketing effectiveness? How do you know that your marketing actions will bring you the most success? How do you know that you are executing the fundamentals of marketing?

Marketing departments and initiatives are run by professionals with diverse backgrounds and experiences. For better or worse, marketing priorities are established and executed based on the collective experience of these professionals. Wouldn't it be ideal to check your fundamentals? The Marketing Diagnostic tool and process is based on proven theory and best practices from the literature and over 100 years of marketing experience.

The Marketing Diagnostic is a tool and process that assesses your current marketing level, assesses your desired marketing level, and sets your top priorities to improve your marketing. The assessment is based on Phil Kotler's marketing audit and publications, a comprehensive literature review, and over 60 years of experience. The assessment covers up to 16 questions areas with 4 answers per question. Your answers will determine where you are today, where you want to be, and your top marketing priorities.

Objectives

The objectives of the Marketing 4Ps Fundamental Diagnostic are to

1. Establish and document your current level of marketing;
2. Establish your desired level of marketing; and
3. Define your top marketing priorities.

Process Description

The organization can use the Standard Marketing 4Ps Fundamental Diagnostic survey or tailor the survey to meet its specific language or needs. The organization attains input from up to 25 marketing and stakeholders from other departments via the Marketing Diagnostic survey. Inputs are

1. An opinion on the current level of marketing for the organization;
2. An opinion on the desired level of marketing for the organization; and
3. The top marketing priorities.

These inputs are averaged for each issue area, analyzed, and delivered in a brief report.

Value of the Diagnostic Survey

The Marketing 4Ps Fundamental Diagnostic Survey provides a systematic review of the organizations' marketing activities focused on high impact marketing priorities with inputs from key stakeholders in the organization. Aligning stakeholder opinions on marketing activities and priorities can improve marketing effectiveness and collaboration with colleagues in sales, research and development, customer service, finance, and other departments. The survey can be repeated quarterly or periodically to measure progress and reassess priorities.

Survey and Instructions

Review the survey and decide to use the existing tool or to tailor the tool to the organization. Invite your colleagues from marketing, sales, research and development, and other functions to complete the survey. If possible, also ask trusted customers to complete the survey. The results can be analyzed and put into a format that includes perspectives from all participants.

Marketing Diagnostic 4Ps Survey

<u>Are today or want to be</u>
Mark the letter that describes where you **are today** and where you **want to** be within 12 months.

Marketing Management

1. Your *market knowledge* includes …
   a. Understanding of demographic, economic, technology, political, cultural, clinical practice, and competitive trends and their impact on your business
   b. "a" plus: Clarity on what additional knowledge will increase your success and actions in place to get this knowledge
   c. "b" plus: Early notice of competitive activities from customers and insights from thought leaders
   d. "c" plus: Improvement of market conditions from your initiatives
2. Your *marketing strategy* has ….
   a. Specific written plans for product, price, promotion, and distribution

b. a plus: realistic strategies, SMART goals, clear competitive advantage, endorsed by key leaders

c. b plus: relevant customer input, contingencies, scorecard driving new tactical actions

d. c plus: cross-functional action plans (who, what, or when) and metrics on with one-page summary

3. Your *marketing metrics* ...

a. Show actual versus plan and variances for sales, expenses, sales pipeline, and progress on the highest priority marketing activities

b. a plus: Measures lead to purchase by lead source (trade show, Web, cold call, advertising, etc.)

c. b plus: Are summarized on one page as a *dashboard*

d. c plus: Systematic pilot programs and analysis of ROI by program cause reallocation of resources

4. Your *cross functional leadership* includes ...

a. No systematic teamwork

b. a plus: effective marketing and sales teamwork

c. b plus: effective marketing, sales, R&D, finance, and manufacturing

d. c plus: product teams with all departments with monthly metric reviews

Product

5. Your *new product and product upgrade pipeline* includes ...

a. Ideas to incrementally upgrade your current products are prioritized

b. a plus: occasional product upgrades and new products launched with inconsistent success

c. b plus: stage-gate new product process with effective process and successful launches

d. c plus: over 30 percent of annual sales from new products

Promotion

6. Your *segmenting and targeting* …
   a. Has not yet determined the most valuable segments and most valuable customers in each segment
   b. Has clearly defined most valuable segments and customers by name
   c. b plus: identifies strategic and manager decision makers, the *fox* (has veto or power to close)
   d. c plus: differentiates selling practices by innovator, early adopter, and majority segments

7. Your *messages* to high-value targets …
   a. Are not effectively moving prospects through the purchase decision process
   b. Clearly and powerfully state your brand promises that answer "why buy from us now?"
   c. b plus: Are proven with evidence,** consistently delivered, and create urgency that closes deals
   d. a, b and c plus: Makes customers say *WOW,* monetizes benefits, neutralizes competitors, and creates dissatisfaction with the present, compelling vision and easy steps to vision

8. Your *message delivery* to high value targets …
   a. Does not have written questions and messages for key decision makers
   b. Has 20 second and 2 minute messages (what you ask and tell) that are continually improved
   c. b: plus: Engages targets in a two-way conversation and effectively moves them to purchase

---

* Evidence: examples for medical device companies: well-designed studies; observational studies; case studies; registry or collection of data; publications; presentations; posters; abstracts; white papers; editorials; testimonials; reference centers; value calculators—versus competition and status quo; promotional videos; user videos.

    d. c plus: Is updated regularly to measurably improve the sales process (leads, proposals, sales)

9. Your *sales pipeline* ...

    a. Is not systematically and consistently reported with clear definition of terms

    b. Is systematically reported by stages with probability percentage, dollars, and timing per opportunity

    c. b plus: Process shares actions that improve awareness, interest, trial, purchase, and repeat purchase

    d. c plus: Data used to drive conversations that increase close rates and shorten sales cycle

10. Your *customer development* in high-value targets ...

    a. Solves problems, ensures smooth operations, and gets early notification of competitive issues

    b. a plus: Increases customer expertise related to your product and application

    c. b plus: Systematically helps customers become recognized experts

    d. c plus: Systematically creates raving fans and drives company improvements

11. Your *proof development* includes ...

    a. Testimonials, references, Web, and materials edited and improved by customers

    b. a plus: case studies and publications: abstracts, posters, presentations, articles, editorials

    c. b plus: value worksheets with data and ability for customer to put in their assumptions versus competition and the status quo.

    d. c plus: well-designed multicenter studies that prove the products' clinical and economic value

12. Your *marketing and sales tools* include ...

    a. Clear, concise, consistent information delivered in the highest impact manner, such as brochures, podcasts, webinars, booklets, pocket guides, posters, and e-blasts

    b. a plus: Proof that the sales team is fully trained and using each tool based on the specific customer situation to advance sales

    c. b plus: Specific promises to the customer of clinical and monetized value in a format (brochure, PowerPoint, etc.) tailored to customer

    d. c plus: Continual improvement of tools based on collaboration with sales team and customers

13. Your *sales training* includes …

    a. Company, product, customer, competitive and market knowledge required for successful sales

    b. a plus: Initial and follow-up training on techniques, processes, and tools that most grow sales

    c. b plus: Use of accelerated learning techniques including video of sales person

    d. c plus: Use of systematic feedback from customers on sales person's strengths and areas to improve

Pricing

14. Your *pricing* is …

    a. Based on history or cost-plus rationale

    b. Tiered to drive larger purchases and purchases based on delivered PO dates

    c. b plus: Based on delivered value (monetized benefits) to the customer and rarely discounted

    d. c plus: Moves customers to most delivered value for them and most profitability for the company

Place (Distribution)

15. Your *distribution system* …

    a. Effectively deliver your products

    b. a plus: Has continual improvement programs for manufacturing, distribution, order processing, and delivery

    c. b plus: Optimizes sales by geography (country, market, and city) using direct sales, distributors, and online channels

    d. c plus: Provides a sustainable competitive advantage and is reviewed regularly

16. What marketing issues not aforementioned are urgent and important? _____

_____

_____

What are your top three priority areas?

1.

2.

3.

Recommended Next Steps

The findings in the report can be discussed with the leaders in the organization to reach agreement on the top priorities and establish actions for each priority. A sample report is shown in Figure 1.3.

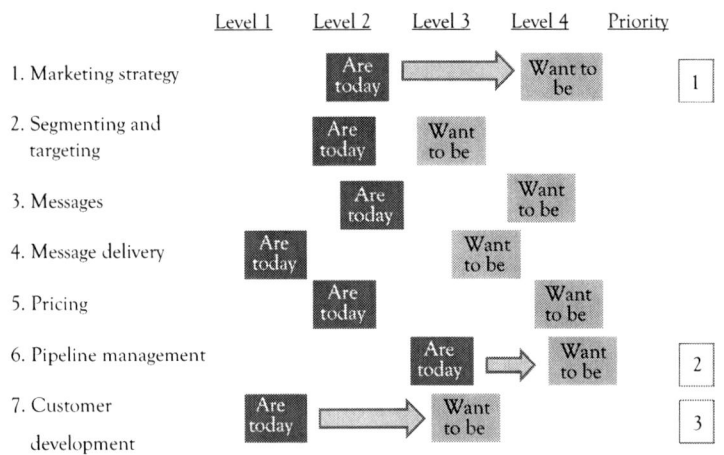

Figure 1.3 Marketing Diagnostic summary

Sidebar #1

Origins and Intent of the Marketing Function

The marketing function was created in the mid-1900s to support the company president by increasing and analyzing customer input or the *voice of the customer,* and systematically integrating the efforts of all functions and extending the reach of the CEO into the organization. The voice of the customer is the useful distillation of all inputs from users and potential users that can help the company succeed. The systematic integration of all functions means comprehensive coordination, leadership, and teamwork with colleagues from all departments (sales, strategy, clinical education, technical support, customer service, manufacturing, quality and regulatory, finance, research and development, etc.) to create and implement plans that exceed company goals. Extending the reach of the CEO is described as follows:

> Marketing will be the basic motivating force for the entire corporation. Soon it will be true that every activity of the corporation—from finance to sales to production—is aimed at satisfying the needs and desires of the consumer. When that stage of development is reached, the marketing revolution will be complete. (Keith 1960)

> John Farley stated: "Marketing's ultimate role in the firm is to drive creation of value for buyers and capture ... a significant part of that created value for the company" (Lehman and Jocz 1997).

Marketing Process

The goal of the marketing process is to optimize value delivered to customers and the organization and its shareholders. Phil Kotler describes the marketing mindset in the form of the formula shown as follows:

R => STP => MM => I => C = Effective, continually improved marketing

Definitions:

R = Research on the market size and company potential

STP = Segmenting, targeting, and positioning the company's products

MM = Marketing mix—allocation of resources and planning for the 4Ps

I = Implementation

C = Control (Kotler 1999).

Effective marketing starts with research that provides deep and broad understanding of the people who the company wants to serve. It continues by segmenting customers into meaningful groups, targeting specific customers by name, and positioning the company such that the reasons to buy are compelling compared with alternatives to the status quo and competitive offers. It creates a plan to optimize profits with allocation of projects and dollars to activities to increase value of the product through the 4Ps: promotion, pricing, product enhancements, and place or distribution.

This process is continuous and occurs for the organization and each product line or product.

Leadership and Management

Product Introduction Team Overview: Team Leader, Teammates, and Senior Management

It is a privilege to be involved with launching a new product. New products can help people live better lives and energize the organization. Company leaders need to decide who will be responsible for preparing for the product launch and how these people will work together. An effective model consists of a product launch team leader who is accountable for all aspects of the project and has a direct connection to senior management.

The team leader's function is to drive the project, delegate tasks, guide analysis, prioritize, and make decisions with input from customers and prospects, all relevant company functions and senior management. Senior management's role is to anticipate and resolve difficult issues, and accept or modify the team leader's recommended actions. Senior management also ensures implementation of recommendations that most effectively and efficiently generate value for customers and shareholders. The company has the highest probability of generating the most value from the new product when senior management and the team leader have a highly effective working relationship.

This sounds basic. Still, many times colleagues will undermine the product launch by not cooperating with the launch team or saying they will do something for the team and then not delivering. Like all projects, there needs to be consistent, repeat messages that require support for the product launch and effective escalation (report to higher authority) of issues to ensure obstacles are overcome immediately.

In most cases, the team leader has full responsibility for the project with no or little formal organizational authority over his or her launch team members. Often, team members formally report to functional managers in other departments and are assigned to the product introduction team on a project basis. The team leader must ensure that multiple launch strategies are considered, prioritized, and decided on at the appropriate time and by the appropriate people in the organization. Of course, this can create issues with colleagues not assigned as the leader. Some team members may not prioritize enough time to this project, some may lack technical or team skills, and some may be jealous of the leader. These potential conflicts need to be addressed through effective team leadership and effective teammate behaviors.

"Sample Team Behaviors"

1. Develop goals and plans
2. Enhance communication among members
3. Develop and maintain positive relationships among members
4. Solve problems and make decisions on a timely basis
5. Successfully manage conflict
6. Facilitate productive meetings
7. Clarify roles for team members
8. Operate in a productive manner
9. Exhibit effective team leadership
10. Provide development opportunities for team members

An important skill for the team leader and team members to develop is running and participating in effective meetings. One characteristic of successful meetings is to define and practice clear meeting ground rules. The following are sample ground rules:

- Cellphones turned off
- Be respectful—no interrupting
- Support and build on ideas from colleagues: "Yes-anding" = use *yes* to affirm, *and* to build
- Everyone is responsible for keep us on track and on time
- If we need to change topic or time, we'll agree as a group on it
- Everyone needs to speak up and share their ideas

Sidebar # 2

Powerful Meetings: "Must-have" Elements and How to Implement Them

> *If you refuse to accept anything but the best, you very often get it.*
> —W. Somerset Maugham

Information on Implementing Meetings Is Vast, Yet There Are Too Few Effective Meetings. Why? There Are at Least four Reasons

1. Creating effective meetings requires preparation and discipline
2. The abundance of poorly run meetings makes people think they are normal
3. Too few people understand that effective meetings are critical to reaching goals and energizing teammates
4. Almost unconsciously, participants keep the status quo in place by complaining and offering no solutions.

So, How Do You Define an Effective Meeting?

To borrow from Phil Harkins book, *Powerful Conversations: How High Impact Leaders Communicate*, an effective meeting results in two of the three elements:

1. The relationship between participants is enhanced.
2. There is an *ah-ha* moment, or a significant discovery is made by each participant.
3. There is an effective action plan where each person publicly commits to at least one specific action by a specific date.

Professional event planners take great care in preparing all aspects of the events and for many contingencies. In business, a relatively small amount of time put into meeting preparation can provide the tremendous benefits of more productivity and energized colleagues.

How Do You Achieve an Effective Meeting? Plan

You can increase your chances of having an effective meeting by reviewing the following checklist that reminds you to pay attention to important elements of successful meeting preparation.

Before the Meeting

- Whoever calls the meeting is or assigns a meeting facilitator and declares the main objective of the meeting as communication, decision making, or other (then specify)
- Meeting facilitator ensures distribution of written and verbal invitations, including time and place, objectives, agenda items, and length of time for each item
- Each invitee responds to meeting facilitator by specified date (e.g., within two days)

- If invitee cannot attend or stay for the entire meeting, he or she notifies the facilitator and sends a representative or written and verbal communication of his or her contributions to the meeting.
- Participants prepare themselves for the meeting (e.g., read relevant materials prior to the meeting and bring relevant information to the meeting)
- Meeting facilitator ensures all required materials are in the room—projector, overhead, flip charts, pens, refreshments, and so on.
- Participants arrive to the meeting before the start time
- Meeting facilitator identifies who are the timekeeper and scribe and defines their roles

During the Meeting

- If possible, the meeting facilitator takes some time to warm the group up with a light-hearted introduction (appropriate joke or quote or story)
- Meeting facilitator reviews aloud objectives, agenda topics, and time allotments and gets agreement or revisions
- Each participant treats colleagues respectfully and offers constructive and positive comments
- Each participant is responsible to keep the discussion on track (*one-minute rule* = if anyone is off the topic for more than one minute, a participant calls for a time-out and ask to refocus on the agenda topic)
- Meeting facilitator manages the time for each topic
- If nonconstructive arguments occur, the meeting facilitator mediates the disagreement or tables it for follow-up outside the meeting
- All participants are responsible for creating a collaborative environment, ensuring input from all participants, and discouraging nonconstructive dominance by any attendee

- Where appropriate, any participant should make proposals and call for votes or consensus
- Spend 5 to 15 minutes to commit to future action plan written clearly in view of all participants. Each person reads aloud their action and delivery date. State when and how the action plan will be reviewed
- When appropriate, have an exit survey that covers topics such as the overall effectiveness of the meeting, what was most valuable, and what needs improvement. Commit to when the action plan will be reviewed, how it will be reviewed, and who will review it

After the Meeting

- Distribute the written action plan distributed to attendees and others if appropriate, with a goal of within one working day
- Distribute the written summary of survey within three working days
- Review the action plan per the commitment made in meeting

How do You Spread the Behaviors of Effective Meetings?

- Exercise authority: You can use authority and influence to increase the effective meeting behaviors. With authority, the superior can declare how to run meetings in the company, and train colleagues on the companies' endorsed methods.
- Lead by visible example: With influence, people lead by example and spreading the methods as others become interested.

How Do You Inspire Behavior Change Toward Effective Meetings?

- Publicly recognize and reward participants:
  - o Create opportunities to praise colleagues who demonstrate behaviors that encourage effective meetings, including simply saying statements such as "thank you for setting the objective and agenda prior to the meeting," writing thank you notes or e-mails, and using your formal recognition and reward system.
- Publicly and gracefully call attention to participants who do not keep a commitment:
  - o These moments of attention might include using specific responses for specific issues. For example, when someone arrives after the meeting time, ask if he or she is committed to arrive on time and charge $1.00 per minute to be put into a pool.
- Measure and report progress at every meeting:
  - o As Bill Hewlett said, "What gets measured is what gets done."

So What Can You Do Right Now?

You can make a powerful, positive difference in your organization by creating your own guidelines and introducing them into your and your organization's daily practices. Your colleagues will eventually follow you, and people interested in increasing the performance of your organization will applaud you. When someone says running an effective meeting is like herding cats, let them know that herding cats is easy when you show them the catnip.*

---

* See http://www.robkanzer.com/news/effectivemeetings.htm

CHAPTER 2

New Product Launch Team Leadership Approach

Never give in—never, never, never, never, in nothing great or small, large or petty, never give in except to convictions of honour and good sense. Never yield to force; never yield to the apparently overwhelming might of the enemy.

A pessimist sees the difficulty in every opportunity; an optimist sees the opportunity in every difficulty.

—Winston Churchill

Introduction

The new product team has the opportunity to orchestrate the introduction of the product to the market. The team can be most effective by following fundamental best practices to create conditions for success, such a clear vision, SMART (specific, measurable, actionable, realistic, time bound) goals, analyzing plans using a change model, and reporting on metrics that matter.

Conditions Required for a Successful Product Introduction

The company needs to create an environment for success. This environment promotes the creation of a clear vision and goals for the new product, resources to fund programs that will increase product usage, effective people in all critical functions, and a winning attitude.

Vision

The team creates a compelling vision that inspires followers and attracts resources to the project. This vision needs to connect with the overall company vision. The product vision describes the aspiration for the product, or what the world would look like when it reaches peak success. The following are the examples of vision.

- Dramatically reduce infection rates
- Dramatically improve the life of every patient
- Cause caregivers and patients say "Wow, my life is much better because of this product!"
- Deliver better quality with dramatically reduced hospital days
- Deliver surgery with no side effects
- Provide the world's best surgery experience

SMART Goals

The vision is supported by *SMART* goals. The following are the examples of SMART goals for the vision *dramatically reduce infection rates*:

- Deliver a new product and training that improve infection rates by 70 percent for 10,000 patients by December 31, 2015.
- Achieve revenue of $15 million, profit of $8 million, five additional points of market share, and 1 percent market growth by December 31, 2015.
- Measure the customer experience weekly and strengthen what is going well and improving deficiencies with systematic quarterly feedback from customers with systematic annual review in December, 2015.
- Prove 30 percent improvements in clinical, ease of use and economic metrics through studies begun by June 15, 2015 to finish no later than June 15, 2017.

Strategy

Often business leaders talk about strategy as if it is a mysterious or magical concept. It is common to hear executives say "we just need a better strategy" without defining the word *strategy*. Strategy is simply a plan that evolves. A strategy evolves to anticipate or react to the changing market conditions as well as competitive and company situations. Ask your product launch team to show you their strategy. You may hear "I'll get that to you soon" or "we are working on it" or you may be handed a long document with massive amounts of data. If you are unable to find a one-page strategy for your new product, then you are in trouble. The one-page document needs to communicate the *must-do* elements of the launch plan, and evolves as the team learns new information and adjusts actions accordingly.

On the way to creating a one-page strategy, the team can create a thoughtful, comprehensive, plan that provides background, data and analysis, insights, and recommendations. The comprehensive plan includes the following:

- Market assessment—size, growth, segments, total and *accessible* customers, SWOT (strengths, weaknesses, opportunities, threats), company and product competitive positioning (shown in 2 × 2 matrixes), and any other relevant analysis
- High-value customer assessment—description and dimensioning of your target customers and product revenue potential for each target segment
- Value proposition—why must the target customer buy from you now?, tailored to strategic, managerial, and operational customer segments
- Fit with the company's existing offerings and specific differentiation from competition
- What you are counting on to win—summary of key product characteristics and company actions that will create success
- New product launch revenue and profit forecasts that identifies incremental revenue and profit if the new product cannibalizes existing products
- Detailed plans for
  - Targeting and measuring sales process
  - Messages and message delivery to target customers, including how monetizing benefits the customer

o Sales force preparation: reward and recognition program including goals or quotas, training program, materials, samples, and so on.

o Promotion plan including advertising, public relations, publications, online activities, national and local industry meetings, engagement of industry leaders, local workshops, national webinars, and collaboration with industry organizations

The team secures organizational support for all recommendations to ensure senior management endorsement. The leaders in the company need to fully commit to implementing stated actions on budget and on schedule. This is time for complete alignment and no dissension within the company. The analogy of a sports season can apply to the product launch process. Each week or month can be considered a game, and the year can be considered a season. Plans with competitive assessments are made, actions are implemented, results measured, and then new actions are created based on new information. There must be a feedback system that gathers and analyzes reasons for higher or lower expected results that engages target customers and company personnel, especially the professionals with high customer contact. Disciplined, honest reviews of results compared to plan are required. Underplan performance needs analysis of reasons for the underperformance and corrective actions. Overplan performance deserves a celebration and can fuel additional actions to accelerate this success.

Resources to Fund Required Programs

The team needs to identify the resources required for all activities. These resources include, and are not limited to, people, expertise, and money to develop and modify the strategy, connect with customers, connect with the sales team and all relevant departments, create promotional materials, training methods and materials, conference *booth* design and creation, sales and clinical training programs, marketing programs, capital equipment, and tools needed for measuring programs, advertising if and where appropriate, web presence, social media, reporting on metrics on interim (such as sales pipeline estimates, customer satisfaction and, product reliability) and monthly, quarterly, and annual results including revenue, profit, and market share.

Team Composition: Effective People in Affected Functions

The team includes professionals from all functions who have a significant stake in the new product introduction. Each team member must have the experience, skills, and authority in their domain to ensure that all of their functional needs are in the team's plan.

In the mid-1990s, we used the following change model to help drive a new marketing and sales approach at the Renal Division of Baxter Healthcare. This model helped explain our successes and diagnose our failures. The model assumes that six factors need to be in place in order to achieve effective, efficient, and lasting change: vision, goals and strategy, skills, incentives, and resources. The potential consequences of missing one of these factors are shown in Figure 2.1. For example, a lack of vision results in confusion and a lack of goals and strategy results in false starts. When all of these elements are aligned, then lasting change can occur.

The product introduction team can use this model to identify strengths and weaknesses and as a framework to reveal where there are gaps and discuss how to fill the gaps.

Key Change elements

_____ + Goals & Strategy	+ Skills	+ Incentives +	Resources	= Confusion
Vision + _____	+ Skills	+ Incentives +	Resources	= False starts
Vision + Goals & Strategy	+ ____	+ Incentives +	Resources	= Anxiety
Vision + Goals & Strategy	+ Skills	+ _____ +	Resources	= Frustration
Vision + Goals & Strategy	+ Skills	+ Incentives +	_____	= Gradual change
Vision + **Goals & Strategy**	+ **Skills**	+ **Incentives** +	**Resources**	= **Effective change**

Figure 2.1 Effective change requires combination of key elements

Source: Adapted from Thousand and Villa (1995).

Three-Step Change Model

An alternative change model uses three steps to plan a persuasion approach for an individual or market segment, or to diagnose why a change did not

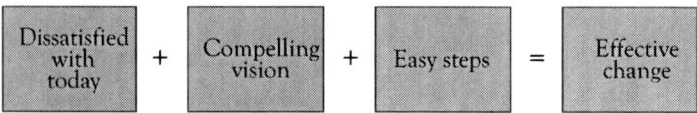

Figure 2.2: Three step change model

Step 1. *Dissatisfied* with today, plus
Step 2. *Compelling vision* of the future, plus
Step 3. *Easy steps* to attain the vision equals
effective, lasting change.

occur. The first step is to assess the dissatisfaction of the current situation. You can create questions that help the individual raise their dissatisfaction such that they desire change. The second step is to provide a compelling vision of the future. You can help the person envision a much better future through a description of the future or *what if* questions that increase the person's desire to attain the vision. The stronger the vision, the more it helps the person increase their dissatisfaction with the present. The third step is easy actions to attain the vision. A change process that effectively addresses these three steps is highly likely to achieve lasting change. Easy steps facilitate the change; difficult steps hinder the change. This *persuasion equation* is shown in Figure 2.2.

You can diagnose any change process by determining what went well and what needs to be improved in each of the three steps. Also, you can organize your questions and messages in a respectful manner for the customer:

1. *Step 1: Dissatisfied with today*: Based on the information that was available at the time, you made a good decision
2. *Step 2: Compelling vision of the future*: Now that there is new, powerful information, it is a good time to consider a new decision
3. *Step 3: Easy steps to attain the vision*: You can easily improve by adopting my solution

Winning Environment–Attitude

A winning attitude is essential. What is a winning attitude? This attitude contains the following characteristics: infectious enthusiasm, positive behaviors, passion, confidence, high energy, frequent words, and actions that help teammates succeed. The professional with a winning attitude

- is curious and continually seeks input;
- looks for new opportunities;
- identifies mission critical problems and works to solve them;
- stays focused on priorities that are in the critical path of project goals;
- is resilient (quickly and powerfully rebounds from setbacks);
- learns from failure and applies the lessons learned; and
- inspires thoughtful actions that ensure achievement of critical path tasks.

When you observe a professional with a winning attitude, you see him or her fully engaged in his or her task. Often, the person is *in-the-flow* and to this person, time seems to fly by. He or she is completely focused on the people on the team and task at hand. He or she is not distracted by unimportant inputs. This person is excited, positive, resourceful, and quite simply, he or she refuses to lose. He or she invites diverse inputs, encourages experimentation, and measures results.

When a team leader shows these qualities, he or she and his or her team spread high levels of energy and inspire confidence to colleagues. We know a winning attitude when we see, hear, and feel it. Anything less than a winning attitude is equally as observable, is equally contagious, and reduces the probability of success.

Metrics

The product launch team defines realistic metrics for success. These metrics track items that will show success, diagnose issues, and help the team prioritize corrective actions. Metrics include sales and gross margin to integrate with the P&L as well as

- A meaningful amount of high-quality feedback (such as number of accounts, usage by account over time, and number of individuals in the account who have used the product);

- Number of new customers per month;
- Number and quality of suggestions for improvement and endorsements;
- Number and quality of testimonials and number of accounts that track clinical and economic value;
- Market share by customer segment; and
- Retention rates by customer segment.

Product Introduction Team: Function and Composition

The product introduction team predicts the date and quantity of first and subsequent product sales. This provides clarity and urgency and helps prioritization of tasks. The product introduction date is an estimate that will move forward or backward depending on many variables. The function of product introduction team is to create and implement strategies and tactics to maximize the products positive impact on customers and the company. This includes analyzing the competitive landscape and company situation to direct and control the introduction.

The product introduction team consists of a designated leader (often a person from the marketing or product development function) and professionals from all relevant functions. The team often has representatives from marketing, sales, clinical education, regulatory, technical services, distribution, product development, and legal and a senior management sponsor. Customer input is sought and analyzed systematically and frequently. In addition, an effective communication plan is set up to inform and solicit feedback from relevant colleagues.

An effective product introduction team shares background information so that all team members understand basic information on the market, competition, customer inputs, and company challenges. First, the team analyzes the money trail. The team needs to clearly understand and document who pays how much for current products and the new product. For a new product to generate sales quickly, it must take market share from an existing product or be compelling enough to attract money from existing budgets. If there is no existing budget that can easily be reallocated to the new product, then a new reimbursement specific to the new product and therapy will be needed for the product to reach its full potential.

Summary

The product introduction team provides the leadership that will rally the people and resources necessary to optimize success. This success depends on answering the following questions:

1. Is the new product vision clear and inspirational to customers and colleagues?
2. Are all of your goals SMART?
3. Is your strategy thorough, thoughtful, and able to adapt as needed?
4. Do you have enough resources?
5. Do you have the required mix of skills?
6. Does your change model analysis conclude that you are well prepared?

CHAPTER 3

Marketing Mix: The 4 P's

Introduction

This chapter covers the 4P marketing framework which is a useful organizing tool to ensure that you are complete and systematic in your new product launch. Additional fundamental concepts to consider include lifetime customer value, the Rogers adoption curve, and an analysis based on *The Tipping Point*. Other critical components of a new product launch include direct selling and a customer service mindset.

Marketing Mix

The product introduction team needs to ensure that all marketing mix options are considered. The traditional 4P—product, price, promotion, and place—framework continues to be an effective and easily understood framework that ensures consideration of activities that can help the product launch.

Product Decisions

All elements of the product need careful consideration so that when taken in their entirety, they compel customers to purchase. "A company aims to make the product or offering different and better in some way that will cause the target market to favor it and even pay a premium price" (Kotler 1999, 97). The product introduction team needs to create the most attractive and profitable mix of product quality, variety, design, features, brand name, packaging, sizes, services, warranties, returns, life cycle management, product portfolio, standard costs and variances, and security of supply chain. This Table 3.1 shows detailed activities for each of the 4 P's.

Table 3.1 The 4P framework

Category	Activities
Product	Quality, variety, design, features, brand names, packaging, sizes, services, warranties, returns, life cycle management, product portfolio, gross margin management including standard costs and variances, security quality, and cost of the supply chain
Price	Pricing strategy—value, penetration, or competitive, list price, volume discounts, event- or date-driven discounts, allowances, payment period, credit terms
Promotion	Segmentation and targeting, sales force (personal selling) composition and management including materials, advertising, sales promotion, public relations, industry conferences, speaker's programs, direct marketing (hard copy and electronic), Web site, online marketing (social media), reference centers, advisory groups, customer and technical service
Place	Channels, coverage, assortments, locations, inventory, transport

Source: Adopted from Kotler (1999, Exhibit 6-1, page 96).

Product Names

The product naming process can be simple or complex depending on the orientation of the leadership team and the influence that the name has on the customer purchase decision. A company can spend a little or a lot of money and time in its quest to find a name that will optimize the products' success. An effective process includes generating names and getting feedback from high-value target customers. Ideally, the name will leverage existing brand equity, convey its unique positioning, imply the brand's benefit, and motivate customers to ask for the product or the treatment. For products and companies new to the market, there are examples of names that do not convey positioning or benefits and over time the benefits are attributed to the product name, for example, Google® and Yahoo®.

Beyond the Product

The product introduction team also creates competitive advantages beyond the physical product, including packaging, additional services, warranties, maintenance contracts, and return policies.

Product Enhancements or Development

If modifications to the product are required in the short term, then the product introduction team provides an analysis of the product's strengths and weaknesses and its opportunities and threats related to the market and competition. Potential modifications are analyzed for their financial impact on the company. This analysis is combined with timing, qualitative benefit, cost, and degree of difficulty for the modification, all of which help set the priority for each modifications. As a part of the product development process, a product requirements document defines features, benefits, and monetized benefits for each modification. There are required (must-have features or the product will not be launched) attributes and desired (features that would increase the product's value and that can be left out if they have significant negative impact on quality, timing, or cost) attributes. As the product goes through the development process, the product introduction team can use this analysis to guide decisions on when to make modifications. For example, a desired attribute can be dropped, whereas an issue with a required attribute could need extra resources and senior management approval.

Market Segments and High-Value Targets

Market segments are groups of customers with similar characteristics. Characteristics can be defined by usage level such as heavy, medium, and light; demographics such as gender, age, and geography; or "reasons for use" such as flying for business, pleasure, or emergency reasons; lifestyle such as soccer moms or pick-up truck macho males; or any other characteristic that will help the company better understand and reach its most profitable customers. Each segment has high-value targets that are institutions or people who bring the most *lifetime* value to the company. *Lifetime value* is defined by the company over a meaningful time period and is often set at three to five years for short-term analysis. Lifetime value is the present value of future profits (revenues minus all costs associated with the individual customer) expected from the customer over the designated time period.

An example of just the financial assessment is shown as follows:

Revenue and profit	
Estimated annual revenues from the customer	$50,000
Estimated number of years of purchases	×5
Total customer revenue	**$250,000**
Company profit margin	20%
Lifetime customer profit $	$50,000
Costs	
Cost of securing this customer for the first purchase	$5,000
Cost to keep and grow this customer per year	$2,000
Number of years	×5
Cost to keep and grow this customer for five years	**$10,000**
Cost over the lifetime of this customer	$15,000
Lifetime customer value (lifetime profit less lifetime costs)	$35,000

Source: Johnston (2009, 79).

Lifetime value is calculated with this type of analysis of potential total company revenue and profit as well as nonmonetary terms such as speaking on behalf of the company, being a reference, giving feedback to improve products, providing testimonials, participating in study development and implementation, writing publications, speaking on webinars, creating podcasts, and any other method that helps the company be more successful.

The most successful launches map high-value organizations and individuals on the Rogers Adoption and Innovation curve to prioritize and use discipline to concentrate on innovators and early adopters while continuing to learn about the different needs of the early and late majority. The organization reaches and focuses on the innovators first, then early adopters, and then the early majority. As you move to the right on the innovation curve, the customer segment often becomes more resistant to change so the messages and objection handling can become more challenging as the company interacts with customers and moves toward the late majority on the adoption curve. For example, innovators may

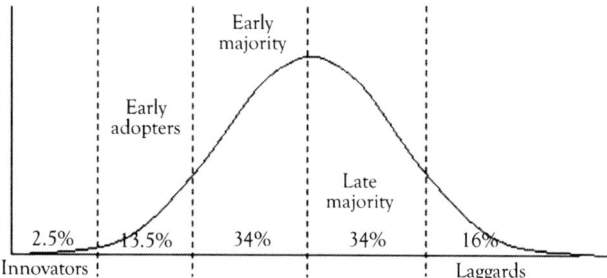

Figure 3.1 Rogers adoption and innovation curve

Source: Rogers (2003).

already be dissatisfied with the incumbent supplier or the status quo and are generally receptive to a new product that can make their lives better. The early majority may have high loyalty to their incumbent provider and may need more compelling clinical and economic data in order to consider a new product and switch from their present situation.

Innovators seek new technologies and take risks that other customer segments would not take in order to be among the first people to try and gain the benefits of new products and services. Early adopters are people, including thought leaders, who want to try new products and services and validate them with careful use or study. The early majority are people who want the benefits of new technologies after they have been confirmed or proven to be useful. The late majority are people who are more risk averse and need more proof before trying the new technology. Laggards are the slowest customer segment to change and may never adopt the new technology.

Thought Leader Roll Out

The thought leader roll-out plan can create significant value for the customer and company. Proving the value of the product with influential people (e.g., heads of training programs, past and future leaders in professional organizations, and high-volume customers) adds credibility to the product due to their respected positions and can accelerate the product introduction. These thought leaders can bring a highly critical yet supportive perspective and help formulate and execute studies that prove the clinical, economic, and quality-of-life value of the product. This approach works best when there are strong personal relationships between the thought leaders and leaders in the company so that expectations are clear and transparent, conversations are open and honest, and responses to issues can be handled within an existing trusted relationship.

Tipping Point Review

In *The Tipping Point*, Malcolm Gladwell described how ideas, diseases, and product adoption spreads. It is useful and informative to assess your strategy against the key factors described in this book. The team analyzes each factor to determine how well it is addressed. If a criterion is not met, then the team can create a plan to fill the gaps. These criteria are as follows.

Connectors, Mavens, and Salesmen

- *Connectors* have ties in many different realms and act as conduits between them, engender connections, relationships, and *cross-fertilization*.
- *Mavens* are people who have a strong compulsion to help other consumers by helping them make informed decisions.
- *Salesmen* are people whose unusual charisma allows them to be extremely persuasive in inducing others' buying decisions and behaviors.

Stickiness

- *A unique quality* that compels the phenomenon to *stick* and influences future behavior. Often counterintuitive or contradictory to the prevailing conventional wisdom.

Context

- *Environment or historical moment* in which a trend is introduced enables the tipping point to be attained.

- *Groups of 150 or less* usually display a level of intimacy, interdependency, and efficiency that begins to dissipate markedly as soon as the size of the group increases over 150 (Gladwell 2002).

Direct Professional Selling

Professional selling is helping the customer improve his or her work life. This can include helping him or her get the job done, keep the job, or get a promotion. Professional selling requires motivating others and includes the following:

- Persuading, influencing, and convincing others
- Convincing someone else to part with resources—time, attention, effort, and money—and leave them better off after the transaction
- Convincing someone else to give up something they value for something you have (Pink)
- "You can have everything you want, if you will just help enough other people get what they want."—Zig Ziglar (2003)

Professional sales people care about their customers, learn what they need and want, take the time to find out what will motivate them to buy, and inspire them to buy from them. Professional sales people have personal face-to-face, phone, and e-contact with customer to move them to an action or purchase that the customer may not have otherwise done.

Sidebar

Congratulations, You're in Sales!
If you think personal selling is only for salespeople, think again. Everyone in every walk of life uses personal selling (some more effectively than others!) Selling is what makes people successful. We all have to sell our ideas, our points of view, and ourselves every day to all sorts of people—and not just those related to our

jobs. For example, when you work on a team project, you have to sell your ideas about how your team should approach the project (or, sometimes more delicately, you will have to persuade others as to what you should do about a lazy team member). When you are with your friends, you have to sell your point of view about which movie you want to see or where you want to go to eat. When you pitch in for a friend's gift, you have to sell your ideas about what gift to give. You are selling every day whether you realize it or not. (Richmond 2002, 10–11)

Professional selling is not

- Misrepresenting the product or company;
- Telling lies or omitting important information about the product or company;
- Manipulating another to buy something that doesn't help them;
- An infomercial or an advertisement or pitching a product.

Professional selling builds long-term relationships and is also called relationship selling. The central goal of relationship selling is:

Securing, building, and maintaining long-term relationships with profitable customers. Relationship selling is oriented toward the long term. The sales person seeks to keep his or her customers so satisfied with the product, the selling firm and the salesperson's own level of client service that they will not switch to other sources for the same products. (Johnston 2009, 5)

This means providing credible, compelling reasons for the customer to buy versus taking no action and versus competitive alternatives. These reasons are included in the "value proposition." Value represents the net bundle of benefits the customer drives from the product you sell and the service you deliver. Value is the total benefit less the total costs to the customer. The net bundle includes price, quality, service, reliability, and the sales person's expertise and problem resolution.

The problem with the phrase value proposition is that there are so many definitions that each business person may perceive a different definition. The question that needs to be answered is simply *why buy from me now?*

The reasons why the customer should buy from you now need to be described in terms of three value categories: (1) raising the customer's revenue, (2) saving the customer's cost and time, and (3) improving the customer's quality of life.

Putting the customer at the center of the firm's attention is a key component of professional selling. Customers pay money for products or services, which makes it possible for the organization to exist. A customer mindset is a requirement for sales people. Descriptors of a customer mindset toward external and internal customers is shown in the following table:

Test your customer mindset

External customers (people who are involved in the process to buy your products)	Internal customers (employees of your company)
I believe that …	*I believe that …*
I must understand the needs of my company's customers	Employees who receive my work are my customers
It is critical to provide value to my company's customers	Meeting the needs of employees who receive my work is critical to doing a good job
I must understand the person who buys my company's products and services	It is important to receive feedback from employees who receive my work
I can perform my job better if I understand the needs of my company's customers	I focus on the requirements of the person who receives my work
Understanding my company's customers will help me do my job better	
Score yourself from 1 to 6 on each item. 1 = strongly disagree and 6 = strongly agree. The higher the score, the higher the customer mindset you've achieved.	

Source: Kennedy et al. (2002, 159–71).

Highly effective sales people make it a habit to use the following seven strategies:

1. Look to the customer for the solution—although product knowledge is important, it is only a baseline, and your solution needs to be tailored to the specific customer need
2. Be committed to presentation improvement
3. Embrace new ideas
4. Focus on helping. Helping is the overarching strategy—the hallmark—of the highly effective salesperson.
5. Possess a vision and attitude focused on customer relationships
6. Think of themselves as marketers
7. Pull customers ever closer to a partnership model in business (Graham 2008)

Sidebar

Profiles of Sales People: Challengers Are the Stars

The Sales Executive Council launched a global study of sales representative's productivity three years ago involving more than 6,000 representatives across nearly 100 companies in multiple industries (by Mathew Dixon and Brent Adamson).

1. *Every sales professional falls into one of five distinct profiles.*
   Quantitatively speaking, just about every business to business sales representative in the world is one of the following types, characterized by a specific set of skills and behaviors that defines the representative's primary mode of interacting with customers:

   • *Relationship builders* focus on developing strong personal and professional relationships and advocates across the customer organization. They are generous with their time, strive to meet customers' every need, and work hard to resolve tensions in the commercial relationship.

- *Hard workers* show up early, stay late, and always go the extra mile. They'll make more calls in an hour and conduct more visits in a week than just about anyone else on the team.
- *Lone wolves* are the deeply self-confident, the rule-breaking cowboys of the sales force who do things their way or not at all.
- *Reactive problem solvers* are, from the customers' standpoint, highly reliable and detail oriented. They focus on postsales follow-up, ensuring that service issues related to implementation and execution are addressed quickly and thoroughly.
- *Challengers* use their deep understanding of their customers' business to push their thinking and take control of the sales conversation. They are not afraid to share even potentially controversial views and are assertive—with both their customers and bosses.

2. *Challengers dramatically outperform the other profiles, particularly relationship builders.*

We found that challenger representatives dominate the high-performer population, making up close to 40 percent of star representatives in our study. What makes the challenger approach different?

The data tell us that these representatives are defined by three key capabilities:

Challengers teach their customers. They focus the sales conversation not on features and benefits but on insight, bringing a unique (and typically provocative) perspective on the customer's business. They come to the table with new ideas for their customers that can make money or save money—often opportunities that the customer had not realized even existed.

Challengers tailor their sales message to the customer. They have a finely tuned sense of individual customer objectives and value drivers and use this knowledge to effectively position their sales pitch to different types of customer stakeholders within the organization.

Challengers take control of the sale. Although not aggressive, they are certainly assertive. They are comfortable with tension and are unlikely to acquiesce to every customer demand. When necessary, they can press customers a bit—not just in terms of their thinking but around things such as price.

3. *Challengers dominate the world of complex "solution selling"*
When we cut the data by complexity of sale—that is, separating out transactional, product-selling representatives from complex, solution-selling representatives—we find that challengers absolutely dominate as selling gets more complex. About 54 percent of all star representatives in a solution-selling environment are challengers. At the same time, relationship builders fall off the map almost entirely, representing only 4 percent of high-performing representatives in complex environments. For any company on a journey from selling products to selling solutions—which is a migration that more than 75 percent of the companies I work with say they are pursuing—the challenger's selling approach represents a dramatically improved recipe for driving top-line growth.*

Transactional Compared to Relationship Selling

Transactional selling is focused on meeting the needs of buyers with little or no attention on creating a long-term relationship. From the customer's perspective, he or she usually does not perceive that the selling organization can add value beyond the basic price, convenience, and acceptable quality of the product. From the seller's perspective, he or she usually wants to quickly persuade the customer to purchase and then move on to the next customer.

Relationship selling includes two fundamental selling concepts: consultative (or solution) selling and enterprise selling. Consultative selling is a discipline that includes skills, strategies, and approaches that help the salesperson to deeply understand the customer's needs and help the customer succeed by using the product as well as services that may or may not be charged to the customer. Consultative selling requires the customer to want to invest time with the salesperson and the salesperson

---

* See https://hbr.org/2011/09/selling-is-not-about-relatio.

to be able to offer ideas that will help the customer and that the customer could not have easily accessed on his own. There is a mutual investment of time and effort by both the seller and the customer. Probing questions and listening are dominant skills in consultative selling. A consultative seller helps the customer in three ways:

1. Understand problems and opportunities in new ways that enable new insights.
2. Arrive at better solutions than they would have discovered on their own.
3. Act as the customer's advocate inside the selling organization to rally resources that can deliver custom solutions tailored to the customer's needs.

Diagnostic tools, sales processes, and other systematic approaches provided by the company can make the consultative salesperson more sophisticated and more successful.

Enterprise selling describes the process of connecting the many people in the selling organization with many people in the customer enterprise. In enterprise selling, the salesperson is the leader who diagnoses what the customer needs and connects the appropriate departments in his or her organization to the appropriate departments in the customer's to maximize value to the customer and to his firm. The enterprise salesperson leverages relevant corporate assets of the selling organization to contribute to the customers' immediate operational and strategic success. An enterprise relationship links both organizations together at multiple levels—CEO to CEO, VPs to VPs, directors to directors, shipping department to shipping department—and all levels in between. They have cross-functional teams with people from both companies and have many people and lots of resources dedicated to helping both organizations become even more successful (Rackham 1999, 25–27).

According to a survey of 134 sales managers, making the transition from transactional to consultative selling is the most frequent challenge faced by sales professionals. The survey asked "What difficulties do your salespeople have in the marketplace?" Results are shown in the following table:

Response	% Responding
Moving to solution—type sell	69
Selling value	67
Inexperience	63
Negotiating	58
Prospecting	55
Closing	55
Unable to get to decision maker	51

"The findings suggest today's sales organization has a more sophisticated focus than a few years ago," said Keith Eades, CEO of Sales Performance International. "While more than half of respondents still cite frustration with basic sales techniques, like prospecting and closing, more encounter trouble at the higher end of the sales process, specifically consultative and value-added selling. This reflects a shift in emphasis as much as the complexity of the tasks involved." Solution selling is where leading companies want to be. Not only does a consultative approach afford a competitive advantage but it also makes for more honorable seller. The salesperson becomes a problem solver and builds a better relationship with the customer. The accepted dogma is don't push product on customers—address their business problem and show value. Frequently, however, sellers have to deal with customers who need to be in control, want to define what they need, and seek the best price. And when all else fails, the seller falls into old habits and ends up shaving the price to win the deal. Effective solution selling requires a culture change, top-to-bottom engagement, and an organization-wide commitment. Otherwise, the organization doesn't speak a common language and gives out different messages (American Salesman 2006).

Another study asked 215 sales managers to rate the importance of 60 key success factors. The following are the top 20 success factors (scale of 1 = no importance at all in hiring decision, 7 = of the utmost importance in hiring decisions).

Score	Skill
6.50	Listening skills
6.36	Follow-up skills
6.32	Ability to adapt sales style from situation to situation
6.11	Tenacity—sticking with a task
6.01	Well organized
6.05	Verbal communication skills
6.00	Proficiency in interacting with people at all levels of a customer's organization
5.98	Demonstrated ability to overcome objections
5.94	Closing skills
5.94	Personal planning and time management skills
5.83	Proficiency in interacting with people at all levels of an organization
5.83	Negotiation skills
5.79	Dresses in appropriate attire
5.72	Empathy with the customer
5.69	Planning skills
5.67	Prospecting skills
5.67	Creativity
5.55	Ability to empathize with others
5.53	Skills in preparing for a sales call
5.50	Decision-making ability

Source: Marshall (2003).

Listening and Questions

Good listeners ask good questions. So "listening skills" is actually "listening and asking skills." Good sales people continually work on creating questions that help them better understand what will most help the customer and validate that their proposal will be accepted by the customer. Listening skills seem basic and easy to implement. However, it can be extremely challenging to consistently use good listening skills to every conversation. These basic good listening skills include the following.

- Truly focusing on the person who is talking.
- Listen to the words, tone of voice, and body language.
- Encourage the speaker to complete and expand on their thoughts and feelings.
- Hear the words and meaning being conveyed, and hear for the overall meaning as well. For example, a customer may say "I have tried to order this product 3 times and was kicked off your web page each time." This means what was said and depending on the tone of voice, may also mean "I am frustrated by your company's inability to help me."
- Demonstrate that you are listening by verbal and nonverbal cues. Verbal cues can be ok, got it, uh huh, yes, or when appropriate asking "can you please tell me more" or "how did that affect you." Nonverbal cues can be smiling, nodding, and leaning forward.
- Listen to understand, do not agree or disagree.

Hear What People Are Really Saying

Research suggests that we remember between 25 percent and 50 percent of what we hear. That means that when you talk to your boss, colleagues, customers, or spouse for 10 minutes, they pay attention to less than half of the conversation. This is dismal! (by James Manktelow and Amy Carlson)

Turn it around and it reveals that when you are receiving directions or being presented with information, you aren't hearing the whole message either. You hope that the important parts are captured in your 25 percent to 50 percent, but what if they're not?

Clearly, listening is a skill that we can all benefit from improving. By becoming a better listener, you will improve your productivity, as well as your ability to influence, persuade, and negotiate. What's more, you'll avoid conflict and misunderstandings. All of these are necessary for workplace success!

About Active Listening

The way to become a better listener is to practice "active listening." This is where you make a conscious effort to hear not only the words that another person is saying but, more importantly, try to understand the complete message being sent.

In order to do this, you must pay attention to the other person very carefully.

There are five key elements of active listening. They all help you ensure that you hear the other person and that the other person knows you are hearing what they say.

1. Pay attention

    Give the speaker your undivided attention, and acknowledge the message. Recognize that nonverbal communication also *speaks* loudly.

    - Look at the speaker directly.
    - Put aside distracting thoughts.
    - Don't mentally prepare a rebuttal!
    - Avoid being distracted by environmental factors, for example, side conversations.
    - *Listen* to the speaker's body language.

2. Show that you're listening

    Use your own body language and gestures to convey your attention.

    - Nod occasionally.
    - Smile and use other facial expressions that support the speaker.
    - Note your posture and make sure that it is open and inviting, sitting up straight and alert.
    - Encourage the speaker to continue with small verbal comments such as yes and uh huh.

3. Provide feedback

    Our personal filters, assumptions, judgments, and beliefs can distort what we hear. As a listener, your role is to understand what is being said. This may require you to reflect what is being said and ask questions.

- Reflect what has been said by paraphrasing. "What I'm hearing is" and "Sounds like you are saying"" are great ways to reflect back.
- Ask questions to clarify certain points. "What do you mean when you say." "Is this what you mean?"
- Summarize the speaker's comments periodically.

4. Defer judgment
Interrupting is a waste of time. It frustrates the speaker and limits full understanding of the message.

- Allow the speaker to finish each point before asking questions.
- Don't interrupt with counterarguments.

5. Respond appropriately
Active listening is a model for respect and understanding. You are gaining information and perspective. You add nothing by attacking the speaker or otherwise putting him or her down.

- Be candid, open, and honest in your response.
- Assert your opinions respectfully.
- Treat the other person in a way that you think he or she would want to be treated.

Be deliberate with your listening and remind yourself frequently that your goal is to truly hear what the other person is saying. Set aside all other thoughts and behaviors and concentrate on the message. Ask questions, reflect, and paraphrase to ensure that you understand the message. If you don't, then you'll find that what someone says to you and what you hear can be amazingly different!

Start using active listening today to become a better communicator, improve your workplace productivity, and develop better relationships.*

Six Questions to Help You with Your Listening Skills: Who?, What?, Where?, Why?, How?, and When?

"I had six serving men. They taught me all I know. Their names are Who, What, Where, Why, How, and When." They can serve you just as they served Rudyard Kipling a hundred years ago. They are ageless. All they need to do what they did for him and countless others is to be used every day.

We are so busy telling people about what we sell and who we are, we lose sight of who they are and what they are *selling*.

Let's find out what is going on in our customers' world before we try to change it. Who is doing what? Where are they doing it, and why? How are they getting it done, by when?

Write out specific informational and directional questions for each sales call. (A directional question is one you think you already know the answer to but is asked to direct the conversation along the lines you hope to take it.) For example, "When is the current contract up?" You know the date, but want to move toward refining next year's specs in your favor! "Who is the most important person in the process?" You know you are talking to them, but they would like to tell you how big they really are.

Use all six serving men every day on every call.

Sales Management Lesson

Few of us ask enough questions. We pride ourselves on being fast on our feet, a quick study, and a quick take. Don't! We have to train our sales professionals to take things a step at a time.

Trial lawyers are taught never to ask a question for which they don't already know the answer to. It is a great technique for building a case. We have to have our people build information on every call, but we also

---

* See http://www.mindtools.com/CommSkll/ActiveListening.htm

have to teach them to direct the interaction of their customers, otherwise they will just be visiting and not selling.

Directional questions are a natural progression of the informational questions we require to be asked on every call. We teach people to test the waters. Now we have to teach them how to jump in with both feet and make things move—often upstream, but that is what we are all paid for!

What directional questions work in your business? Don't ask your sales reps to make a list. You do it! You are sitting there on all those dual sales calls dutifully keeping your mouth shut, as you are supposed to, but that doesn't mean that you should not be fully engaged. What questions are being asked that are moving the process along? (Hopefully, there are some, and usually with your best people there are.) After the call, compliment the user originator, but then write them down.

If you are to head a sales force, you have to give them direction and also a means to get there. Directional questions are tools of the trade. They are best used, not generically, but rather as specific tuned queries that are professionally meaningful to customers (Falvey 2014).

Follow-up Skills

Follow-up is evidence that you care. At the end of your conversation, declare an action and do it. Continue to find ways to follow-up in ways that help your prospect or customer. This can include completing an action that you declared, bringing new information about the market or competition to the customer, or sharing information that you think the customer would find helpful even if it is not directly related to your business relationship. The key is to declare what you will do by when, then do it. Set and beat expectations. Each commitment that is delivered increases trust and builds the relationship between the salesperson and customer.

Sidebar

Underpromise and Overdeliver

One of the tenets of selling is establishing trust and setting expectations. The best sales people underpromise and overdeliver. In other words, they say that they will do something by a certain day, and then not only do they do it, but they also deliver it one day early. Here is a way to think about the power of this approach: If you order a new pair of jeans online and the estimated date of deliver is Tuesday, but you receive them on Monday, you are delighted. You are pleased that they came early. However, if the jeans were promised for Tuesday delivery, but they arrived on Wednesday, you would be disappointed and probably would not trust that websites for the timely delivery in the future. You can imagine how this strategy builds trust with customers—not only can you rely on the sales person to do what he or she said, but he or she never lets you down and even delivers earlier than promised sometimes. That is how trust is built between salespersons and customer, and the relationship goes to the next level: partnership (Richmond 2010, 67).

Ability to Adapt Sales Style from Situation to Situation

Different customers respond to different styles. Effective sales people learn how to read the room or assess how the conversation is going and adapt so the conversation focuses on mutual benefits. Advanced sales training often includes profiling the customer through personality types, or personas, and developing strategies to more effectively communicate with the customer depending on their style. Two of these profiling systems are DiSC and Myers-Briggs. The DiSC approach is a personal assessment tool and recommended behaviors used to improve work productivity, teamwork, and communication. The DiSC program requires completion of a series of questions that produce a detailed report about your personality and behavior. The program can help sales people better understand your natural style, the natural styles of others, and how to adapt your style to be more effective with any style. DiSC stands for the four styles: dominance, influence, steadiness, and conscientiousness.

Tenacity—Sticking with a Task

The process of developing and strengthening relationships can be long and require a lot of work before seeing tangible rewards such as a purchase. The sales person may need to advocate for the customer within his or her company to ensure that the customer's needs are met. The sales person may encounter many challenges and setbacks along the way, and he or she needs to persevere as long as the potential benefits to the company and sales person outweigh the potential costs.

Summary

New product launch success depends on consideration of fundamental ideas such as the 4P marketing framework, lifetime customer value, the Rogers Adoption Curve, analysis based on *The Tipping Point*, direct selling, and a customer service mindset. Success depends on how well you answer these questions:

1. How well have you addressed the relevant items for your new product in the 4P framework?
2. What is the lifetime value of your target customers?
3. What are the profiles of your customers who are innovators and early adopters? How are you reaching these customers?
4. What is your direct selling approach?
5. What is the status of the customer service mindset in all relevant functions?

CHAPTER 4

Messaging, Professional Selling, Raving Fans, and Customer Development

One can never consent to creep when one feels an impulse to soar.
—Helen Keller

Do not follow where the path may lead. Go instead where there is no path and leave a trail.
—Muriel Strode

Introduction

The new product launch needs to develop messaging, professional selling basics including the sales approach, negotiating techniques, and closing techniques and provide the details on best practices for the new product to the sales team. There needs to be a systematic plan to develop customers and create raving fans.

Messaging

You've got to be believed to be heard. To get your message across, you must first make an emotional connection by appealing to the first brain of your listener. The first brain is the part of our brain that makes the snap judgment to trust or not trust. As babies, we learn about the world from facial expressions, energy, sound, tough, motion, and gestures. As adults, we continue to read and react to these cures.

A speaker's goal is to influence the listener to *buy* his or her ideas. Our success as a communicator comes from

- Being perceived as trustworthy;
- Being perceived as warm, confident, strong, empathetic, and composed.

People buy on emotion and justify with fact. We may think that we buy based on logical reasons, but usually limit our choices through logic and then we make a preconscious emotional buying decision and then justify it with reasons.

To motivate, influence, or persuade face-to-face human communication is most effective. You will be less effective if you are perceived to be evasive, boring, or cold. You will be more effective if you are perceived to be honest, friendly, and warm. We tune into the speaker's message based on these impressions first, not factual content.

When you make eye contact, you appear more confident and less nervous and you can read your listener's reactions. Darting eye movements or closed eyes tend to make listeners less comfortable and they tune out. Upright poster and natural movement convey confidence. Stand tall with shoulders back and stomach in, avoid rocking or standing back on one hip which literally distances you from listeners. Controlled movement conveys energy, enthusiasm, and confidence and helps make an emotional connection with listeners (Decker 2008).

Robert B. Cialdini spent three years going *undercover* applying for jobs and training at used car dealerships, fund-raising organizations, and telemarketing firms to observe real-life situations of persuasion. The book reviews many of the most important theories and experiments in social psychology. Harvard Business Review lists Dr. Cialdini's research in *Breakthrough Ideas for Today's Business Agenda*. The following are Dr. Cialdini's six key principles of influence.

Reciprocity—People tend to return a favor, thus the pervasiveness of free samples in marketing. The person receiving the free sample or gift is usually taught by the culture that he or she is indebted to or positively oriented to the giver.

Commitment and consistency—If people commit, orally or in writing, to an idea or a goal, they are more likely to honor that commitment because of establishing that idea or goal as being congruent with their self-image. Even if the original incentive or motivation is removed after they have already agreed, they will continue to honor the agreement.

Social proof—People will do things that they see other people are doing. For example, in one experiment, one or more confederates would look up into the sky; bystanders would then look up into the sky to see what they were seeing. At one point, this experiment is aborted, as so many people were looking up that they stopped traffic.

Authority—People will tend to obey authority figures, even if they are asked to perform objectionable acts.

Liking—People are easily persuaded by other people whom they like. Cialdini cites the marketing of Tupperware in what might now be called viral marketing. People were more likely to buy if they liked the person selling it to them. Some of the many biases favoring more attractive people are discussed.

Scarcity—Perceived scarcity will generate demand. For example, saying offers are available for a *limited time only* encourages sales (Wikipedia Robert Cialdini 2014).

Description of Relationship Selling

As Daniel Pink explained, selling is moving someone to part with resources—time, attention, effort or money—for something you have—idea, product, or service—so that both people get what they want. Relationship selling is the process of learning what will make your customer's life better and helping him or her improve. *Better* can be defined as more financial rewards, higher quality of life, and more convenience. Relationship selling assumes multiple interactions and relationship growth over time. Transactional selling is an exchange of products or services for money with no expectation of repeat business.

What's in It for Them If They Buy? If You Don't Know, Why Should They?

Getting into benefit selling from feature selling is a big step forward. Just because the link between the feature and benefit seems obvious doesn't mean that the prospect will make that connection. "What this will do for you is …." Taking all this to the next level requires that you identify which benefit will be most important to your specific prospect for this specific situation and sale. Everyone has a little different set of objectives and subjective requirements. The more you know about what they are after (and they will tell you), the more likely you are to be able to lead with the benefit most important to them and thus build the sale on that key point. Jack Lacy called it *hot button* selling. The challenge is not in pushing the hot button, but finding out what and where it is. Once you get a hint of what is important, merely rank order your benefits accordingly. Always begin with your strongest point which, of course, could be a different point for almost every sale. Ask yourself the questions, "What is the most important factor in this prospect's make-up?" "What can I offer that matches up against that perceived need?" "What other benefits support the main message?" When you realize no two sales calls are alike, you will begin to gain great personal benefits as a result (Falvey 2014).

Objection Handling

Objections are reasons why the customer does not want to buy the product. Nearly all products have something that merits an objection. The salesperson needs to be aware of the reasons why the customer may not purchase his or her product and have a thoughtful response prepared for each objection. The buyer does not need a product that meets 100 percent of his or her needs. The buyer needs the product to be above a threshold that makes his or her investment worth it. A useful technique is to adopt the philosophy of *51 percent wins* or that at 50 percent, there is no sale and all you need to do is help the buyer see that it is better for him or her to buy than to pass up the opportunity. This assumes that the product will not and does not need to satisfy all of the buyers' needs, rather the product will satisfy just enough of the buyers' needs to warrant the purchase.

In order to close a sale, the successful salesperson ensures that the customer has shared his or her opinion of the product and has the experience of being heard. The salesperson will ask the customer if he or she is ready to move forward. If the customer says no, then the salesperson asks for the reason. The customer will state his or her objection and the salesperson will repeat or paraphrase so that the customer is validated and so it is clear that the sale person clearly understands the objection. Then the salesperson asks "is there anything else" or "is there any other reason why we wouldn't move forward?" Once all objections are surfaced, then you can ask the customer to help you put them in priority order and work to overcome each objection to help the customer move forward.

Closing Techniques

Closing means gaining a commitment. Typically, we associate closing with a commitment for or physical act of the purchase of a product. Closing can also be a commitment to an idea, to another meeting, to bringing the proposal to another person, or to signing an agreement.

Successful salespeople use many different closing methods depending on the situation. There are seven common closing techniques:

1. Assumptive close: Salesperson verbalizes that he or she assumes that he or she has closed the deal.
2. Minor point close: Salesperson focuses on a small element of the decision. You agree on something small that reflects commitment to the purchase
3. Alternative choice close: Close to minor point close, focuses buyers on minor points; adds a twist of giving prospect options
4. Direct close: Salesperson directly asks buyer for order. Very effective when you're getting strong buying signals (which we will talk about next)
5. Summary of benefits close: Relatively formal way to close. Reviewing some or all of the benefits accepted, reminding buyer of why benefits are important, and then asking direct close question
6. Balance sheet close: (the office) Salesperson helps buyer see pros and cons of placing order
7. Buy-now close: Creates a sense of urgency with buyer that if he or she doesn't buy now something valuable will likely be lost

There are many variations on these techniques. One book describes 365 closing techniques, however they are derived from the preceding seven techniques or they relate to highly specific situations that are not easily generalizable.

Buying Signals

Buying signals are behaviors that indicate that the buyer is interested in purchasing. They include (and are not limited to) when the buyer

a. Replies to your communication (e.g., replies to an e-mail or tweet or returns a phone call)
b. Accepts your offer for a scheduled phone call or meeting
c. Gives positive feedback
   i. Verbal: saying yes, looks good, interesting, and any friendly or supportive words
   ii. Nonverbal: nodding the head up and down, leaning forward, reaching toward you, relaxed posture, bringing out paperwork to consummate purchase, makes positive gestures or expressions, picks up sample and tests it, or examines your literature
4. Asking questions about your product, company, or you
5. Seeking opinions from other colleagues so that you can address their concerns
6. Providing purchasing requirements

These buying signals will help you understand how the sale is going and help you adjust your approach. They will also help you identify what kind of closing techniques might be best for the situation. For example, if the buyer is giving positive feedback and is relaxed, friendly, and open, maybe you can use a direct close. If they are seeking other opinions from their colleagues, you may use a summary of benefits close to remind them of what they will be receiving so that this information is highlighted in their mind when they relay information to colleagues.

Customer Buying Process

The product introduction team needs to provide a framework of the customer buying process that can be modified to the local selling situation.

This customer buying decision process consists of the following stages, with variations for each institution.

Stage one: anticipation of recognition of problem or need

Stage two: determination and description of the traits and the quality of needed item(s)

Stage three: search for and qualification of potential suppliers

Stage four: acquisition and analysis of proposals or bids

Stage five: evaluation of proposals and suppliers

Stage six: selection of order routine

Stage seven: performance evaluation and feedback (Johnston 2009, 57)

When defining the buying process, one needs to consider everyone involved with the purchase decision. Key people in the prospects organization often include initiators, users, influencers, gatekeepers, the buyer, decider, and controller. The product introduction team needs to develop the approach and messages to engage with each department and level (i.e., operational, management, strategic) and type of person (e.g., research and development, manufacturing, marketing).

Many institutional buying processes have one person who can veto or dominate the decision process. One consultative sales training method calls this person the *fox*. The selling process needs to include identifying the fox and working with his or her colleagues to ensure that the fox supports buying your products now. Some institutions have a defined request for proposal process. Some institutions will not declare or even understand their own buying process. Nonetheless, the product introduction team needs to define its best understanding of the buying process for high-value targets so that all team members can keep the customer and competitive dynamic in mind as they plan the introduction.

Initiators perceive a problem or an opportunity and start the buying process for a product or service for their company. The initiator can be at any level in the organization, from a senior manager who is looking for a strategic advantage to an operator who sees how the work can be done better.

Users work with the product or service and often influence the purchase decision.

Influencers give input to evaluating alternatives and help determine specifications for the product and criteria for selecting a new product. They are often technical experts and managers of the department making the purchase.

Gatekeepers control access to others in the purchasing process. They can limit or speed access to people and can control information going to others. They can be *screeners* such as office managers who can block or facilitate access or *filters* such as purchasing agents who may create the worksheets that show comparisons of alternatives.

The *buyer* contacts the selling organization to place the order. The buyer can be the negotiator or can implementing the results of a negotiation.

The *decider*, or the fox, has the final authority to make the purchase. This person may have hierarchical authority or may be a trusted advisor of the hierarchical authority. In either case, this person can veto or push through the decision.

The *controller* manages the budget and tracking for the purchase. This person monitors actual compared to budget performance.

The buying process can have one or multiple people in these roles. In addition, one person may play multiple roles. The salesperson needs to learn the customers buying process and people performing each function to help guide his or her actions.

The company needs to define and create a process to measure and improve the selling process. The following are the six steps in sales process.

- *Awareness* in the product and company
- *Interest* to learn more about how the product can help the customer
- *Try* the product to ensure it delivers the brand promise (or make a commitment if trying the product is not realistic)
- *Buy* from the company
- *Repeat buy*: Buy more of the same products and additional products and grow the relationship with the company
- *Creation of raving fans* for the company

Vignette

Selling Is Not Difficult. Finding Someone Who Wants to Buy Is Difficult

In some businesses, people call in to become new accounts. In most businesses, prospecting and qualifying are the norm. It's a great deal of work. You must kiss many frogs to find the prince, as the saying goes. Few people enjoy *dialing for dollars*, yet those who don't do the hard work of business development seldom reach the levels of those who do. The rule must be: I will make time each day to follow up leads, make cold calls, and pick up the 500-pound phone one more time, or 50 more times, as the case may be. If there were a way around all of this, it would have been discovered long ago. It is true that once you become established, referrals will become a larger and larger source of new business. "Charlie asked me to give you a call" is far easier to say than, "This will only take a minute or two; may I ask you a couple of questions?" An analysis of past successes will soon tell you that new business comes from all the wrong places at all the wrong times—wrong in the sense of the least likely time and places. Your job is to be in the right place at the right time. Prospecting and qualifying will assure that you not only will be paid, but that you will be better paid than most as a result. The law of cause and effect has never had a clearer-cut illustration than the ratio between sales and sales effort. Looking for customers increases the likelihood you will find them. Not easy to do, but very easy to understand. Now go do it.

Sales Management Lesson

One of the worst features to come out of the attempt to computerize sales management has been automated lead follow-up programs. To send your greatest lion hunters running from rat hole to rat hole, isn't what you should be doing. Have a junior staff person, office temporary, or an outside provider do some basic qualifying of all leads before you offload them onto your field sales professionals. You might even give a call to what appear to be hot leads and qualify a few yourself before you pass them on. Once again, the sales management lesson must be one of the positive reinforcement. Who is getting business out of aggressive prospecting and qualifying? That is a story that must be told. What are they doing specifically, in detail? Why is it working for them? Take what works and be sure everyone knows about it. Only a few selected person will understand the sales rewards of prospecting and qualifying and act accordingly. Everyone else will require some kind of management leadership to get and keep him or her moving down the productivity path. You seldom get what you don't ask for. Ask for a high level of sales activity and assure that industry-appropriate efforts are being expended. Don't forget that business development within existing accounts qualifies as prospecting and qualifying. What piece of the pie is missing? Can we get it or at least a bite or two of it? We already know a great deal about our existing accounts, so building on that knowledge and hopefully on past performance, we ought to be able to find the person who can say yes to new business.

We all know that business goes south on occasion, and there may be little we can do about it. One thing we can definitely have an impact on is new business coming in. Be sure to take note of activity levels, and be sure that all know you are doing so. New business development can be just like opening presents. You never know what it will be. If it's a lump of coal, throw it on the fire and open the next gift-wrapped box. Make sure that approach is understood by your field salespeople (Falvey 2014).

Professional Selling Fundamentals

Prospecting and Precall Planning

How do you find a customer? First, you have a lead which is the name of someone who may potentially purchase or influence a purchase from you. A lead can also be called a prospect. The next step is to turn the prospect into a qualified lead or prospect by determining if the prospect meets specific criteria that correlate with people who purchase from your company.

The following are the common qualifying questions:

1. Does the prospect appear to have a need for your product?
2. Can you effectively contact and carry on a conversation (face to face, phone, and electronic) with the prospect?
3. Does the prospect have significant influence on the purchasing process?

4. Does the prospect have the financial capability to make the purchase?
5. Does the prospects company fit the profile of your company's high-lifetime-value customers?

Depending on response to these and other questions specific to the company and industry, the salesperson can categorize prospects into A, B, and C according to attractiveness and allocate efforts in proportion to the potential of the prospect.

Some markets have data on product usage that helps them segment prospects more precisely. For example, pharmaceutical companies can get data on total and new prescriptions by physician. They categorize physicians into 10 categories, or *deciles*, and combine this data with other factors to focus sales representatives on the highest-value prospects. Other factors include thought leadership, influence on peers, tendency to take on new products, and level of managed care influence. Combining the quantitative with qualitative information can guide the sales representative to approach the physicians who are most likely to buy large quantities of the product.

Prospects can be found from many sources. Existing customers can refer you to their colleagues. When you have a good relationship with a customer, you can ask "who do you know who could benefit from our products?" or "if you were me, who else would you talk to?" Prospects can be from your friends and family, social media contacts, professional group members, professional conferences, purchased lists, and other sources.

Prospects come from networking. Networking is creating relationships with people who can help you in your career. The most effective way to create a relationship is to help the other person. When you are in a situation where you can meet other people, adopt the mindset of helping the other people get what they want. This approach requires that you learn what the other person is looking for and that you listen carefully and ask questions that help your learn their needs. Then you can brainstorm with the other person on ideas that can help them. You focus on what the other person is looking for and how you will help them find it. In the course of the conversation, you can share what you want. Be sure to have a short introduction stating who you are and a question or statement that helps the other person understand why they should want to talk with you more about doing business with you.

Conversations with Customers

Conversations with customers help you discover their unique needs, how they operate and how your products fit into their business. Salespeople use this information to match the customer's needs to the company's offer. For each customer interaction, have goals. Ask and answer for yourself: "What do I want to accomplish on this sales call?" The following are sample goals:

- To discover the real customer needs and understand which are most important and ideally their priority order
- To learn who is involved in the decision process and how the process is expected to unfold
- To learn about what the customer likes and would like to see improved about his or her situation
- To verify that the customer is aligned with your company's philosophy and offerings
- To understand the overall goals of the customers and brainstorm how you can help him or her achieve those goals
- To gather information that you can put into a formal sales proposal that clearly states how you will help the customer
- To present information on a product and get feedback from the customer
- To gain agreement for a follow-up meeting with additional people
- To gather information on how the customer plans to use the product so that you can calculate additional revenue or cost savings by switching to your product
- To *read the wall* or notice what the customer has on his wall or on his or her desk so that you can ask questions about what is important to him
- To move the purchasing process to the next step
- To define the specifics of an order

- To gain customer commitment to send the order for approval
- To close the sale and get a signature on an order form
- To deliver new information that will help the customer improve his or her business whether or not it directly relates to your company's products

After the sales objectives are defined, then prepare for the sales call by deciding what you need to ask or send to the prospect prior to the call, what you want to use during the visit, and what you want to leave behind after the visit. In some cases, many visits will be required with many different people in the company in order to accomplish one goal.

Interview with Mr. Randy Dorn, Division Vice President, Allied Barton Security Services, San Antonio Texas:

What do you think are the most important characteristics of a successful sales presentation? It is important to understand the customer's needs and to develop a presentation that communicates how we will address those needs. An effective sales presentation must:

- Demonstrate knowledge of the client's unique needs;
- effectively convey the business outcome the company will achieve by using us;
- Communicate the customized solutions that we will bring to address their needs and ensure that the business outcome is achieved; and
- Provide documented evidence, in the form of case studies or other proof, that demonstrate how we assisted other customer with similar needs.

It is very important to do up-front research on the company you are presenting to and to understand the challenges and mandates that the decision makers have. It is critical to have a relationship with the prospective customer long before a formal presentation may be requested. It is during this early relationship building that the real selling takes place. The prospect must see our business as one that addresses their needs, not our own needs. The relationship involves a consultative approach that educates the prospect on how they can improve profits and productivity, while we add value in areas of their business that we are best suited to affect. We need a clear understanding of their goals, strategies, visions, and mandates. It is though a close relationship that we get to know the customer well enough to understand how we can make a significant impact (Johnston 2009, 164).

Sales presentations are critical events. They are most effective as part of an ongoing conversation between the salesperson and the people in the company who influence and make the purchase decision. Characteristics of a great sales presentation include the following:

1. Makes it clear that you understand the detailed needs of the customer, their business and their specific context in their market
2. Explains the value proposition or the value that is added by our company. Because a common definition of *value proposition* is elusive and often does not get agreed to by the group in a presentation, or even between two people, I prefer answering the question "why buy from me now?"
3. Declares clearly and specifically the advantages and monetized benefits of the product and company
4. Makes it clear what you are offering and how the customer will integrate it into their company
5. Increases the customer's knowledge and interest in the company and products
6. Creates a memorable and positive experience.

To help you prepare for a presentation, you can use these questions:

- What can I tell the customer what will validate that I understand his or her needs, business, and context in their market?
- Why should the customer buy from me now?
- What are the advantages that matter most to the customer and how do I show the monetized benefits of working with us?
- What are the specifics of my offer and how will the customer use it?

- What can I share about my company that will be of interest to the customer and help him or her think more positively of my company?
- What can I do or say that will create a memorable, positive experience and reinforce the main take-aways that I would like the prospect to be able to explain to her colleagues?

Effective professional salespeople tailor their *presentation* to the situation. A formal presentation with handouts can include a PowerPoint or keynote presentation, video, brochures, sample product, full size products, and any tool that helps powerfully and quickly teach the customer how the salesperson can help him or her. The mix of talking and listening will vary based on the planning and implementation of the meeting. A well-prepared presentation that was designed for the salesperson to talk 75 percent of the time may switch to a session where the salesperson listens 90 percent of the time because the opening question such as *what would you like to talk about today?* may take the conversation to unexpected topics. For example, I witnessed one highly effective sales presentation that began with the salesperson asking *what are your issues and how can I help you,* led to the prospect talking 90 percent of the time for two hours, and concluded with a commitment to a $300,000 consulting project.

When things go wrong, adjust. If you had planned for a 30-minute visit and the customer changed it to 15 minutes, then modify your approach. You may ask the customer to choose from the three topics that you wanted to discuss and focus on those with most mutual interest. It is best to have a backup plan for your presentation materials. For example, if you are using a projector, bring hard copies also in case the projector fails. If you are doing a demonstration and your product could fail, bring a backup product. If the customer needs to take an unexpected call or a break, then patiently wait until the break is over and you have the customer's full attention, then recap and proceed. For example, you may recap with something like "I believe that we were talking about options to help you get the functions you need from your customer relationship management system, is that correct?"

Engaging the prospect requires premeeting, meeting, and postmeeting planning and actions.

Premeeting planning includes the following:
Plan for the best first impression possible

- Who do you want to contact prior to the meeting and what do you want to ask or tell them or send to them?
- What coaching can you get from your advocate that will help you prepare for the meeting?
- How early do you want to arrive to ensure that you have the room arranged, handouts in place, and technology is set up for the best first impression?

Behaviors at the meeting include the following:

- Greeting each participant and keeping your focus on discovering and meeting the needs of the customer(s), engage in an appropriate amount of *small talk* or discussion of non-controversial topics such as traffic, weather, where you live, or the local sports or news to *break the ice* and establish safe conversation.
- Ensuring brief introductions of all participants.
- Declaring meeting goals and agenda and modifying if needed.
- Following the advice of the customer who is leading the meeting to ensure you cover the topics of greatest interest and move at a pace that is effective for this particular meeting.
- Per your preparation, ask questions and exchange information with the participants.
- Taking notes so you have accurately understood the customers' needs and questions and catalog follow-up actions.
- Recapping the meeting with key points and next steps—who does what by when.

Postmeeting actions include the following:

- Immediate follow-up to thank the participants for sharing their time and ideas.
- Specific follow-up that you committed to at the end of the meeting including sending an e-mail that states key points and the action plan.

Sample: Follow-up e-mail

Dear Dr. Johnson,

Thank you for sharing your time and ideas with my colleagues and me yesterday! It was a pleasure meeting you and your team.

My notes show that:

- Your goals include growing your skincare product offerings; and
- You would like to do a 15 day trial of our products and test how patients perceive their advantages.

Next steps:

What	Who	By when
1. Complete the opening order form	Dr. Johnson	September 15
2. Deliver products, brochures and posters	John Smith	September 20
3. Perform 1 hour staff training	Jill Jones	September 22

Please let me know if I need to modify anything aforementioned to be more accurate or complete, and let me know if you have comments or questions. Thank you!

Best wishes,

Paul

Building the Relationship

Relationships grow and strengthen when both parties enjoy seeing each other and look forward to their next contact. From the salesperson perspective, this means bringing something valuable to each customer interaction and leaving the interaction so the customer desires to see the salesperson again. The path to continued sales' success includes a nonstop virtuous cycle of identifying and satisfying customer's needs.

Table 4.1 describes how to identify and satisfy customer needs in three steps.

Ask Questions to Identify Customer Needs

The most effective salespeople ask questions. These salespeople use trial and error to find and refine questions that help them discover more information as well as questions that help direct the customer to their solutions. There are several types of questions.

Unrestricted or nondirected or open-ended questions: These questions impose few limitations and draw out as much information as the customer will share. These questions encourage conversation and relationship building, facilitate follow-up questions, and take relatively more time than restricted questions. Examples: What is going well? What would you like to see improved? Why are you moving in that direction?

Restricted or directed or closed questions: These questions require very short or yes or no answers. They direct the customer to a specific response, take relatively little time, and can be effective for gathering facts. Examples: Do you carry this product? How many machines do you currently have?

Questions can be used to collect facts and investigate and validate customers' opportunities or challenges.

Table 4.1 Steps to understand and satisfy customer needs

Step	Actions
Identify customer needs	Ask questions Actively listen
Apply your knowledge to customer needs	Educate the customer on features, advantages, benefits, and value (monetized benefits) Bring a new solution that the customer could not have otherwise known about
Satisfy customer needs	Customer agreement Clear steps forward

Source: Johnston (2009, 175).

An established description system that helps you create effective questions is the SPIN approach. It categorizes questions into four types: situation, problem, implication, and need-payoff questions.

Situation questions find facts about the customer's situation. For example, "how many employees work for you?" The more you can learn these facts via other means such as online sources, the more prepared you are to progress to more valuable questions.

Problem questions ask about the customer's problems, challenges, or dissatisfactions. For example, "Can you please tell me about one of your most challenging issues?" or "When that problem occurs, how does it affect your entire team?" or "What keeps you up at night and why?" These questions are important to use to discover, validate, and prioritize the customer's issues.

Implication questions ask about the consequences and implications of the customer's problem. Once you have defined a high-priority problem, then these questions help the customer think about its implications. For example, "When the delivery is late, how does it impact all the departments in your company and your customers?" or "How does that problem affect you, how does it make you feel?" These questions can teach you about the total impact of the customer problem and build rapport with the customer because these questions require thoughtful answers. These questions can escalate the size and urgency of the customer problem and set the stage for your proposed solution. The larger the implications, the more valuable the solution.

Need-payoff questions ask about the value or usefulness of the proposed solution to the customer's problem. For example, "If you were able to have your deliveries 3 days earlier, how would that impact your work life?" or "If we could help you increase your revenues by 10 percent, how would that help you meet your goals?"

The most effective salespeople create questions tailored to their market, their offering, and their customer's specific needs. In addition to the specific types of questions in the SPIN approach, open-ended questions go a long way in learning from and building a relationship with the customer. Some of these types of questions are "What do you like best about your job, this company, or this product?," "What would you like to see improved?," "Are you ready to move forward?," "What else do you need

before you would like to move forward?," "What else is on your mind?,"
"If you were the VP of Marketing for our company, what would you do?,"
or "If you were me, who would you talk with?"
(See Appendix 4: "Do Questions Really Make the Sale")

Win–Win Negotiating

Negotiation is the act of *conferring with another so as to arrive at the settlement of some matter* or *arranging for or bringing about through conference, discussion and compromise.* The focus is on discussion and compromise is implied. Negotiation is used to tailor your offering to the customer's specific needs and work through customer objections.

In your overall interactions with customers, be sure to create strategies to address these five main customers' concerns:

Do I need your product? The customer must see a clear, convincing, urgent reason(s) to buy your product. If they don't, then they won't buy.

Do I trust your company? The customer may have negative history with your company, or concerns that your company may not stay in business or keep their representative so they would need to switch companies again. The customer may be loyal to their existing supplier and need powerful reasons to switch.

I don't really know you. The customer may be happy with their current situation and representative, wonder if you will be with your company for months or years, or not have a track record of trust with you. The more you can help the customer trust you through your actions and third party endorsements or mutual friends, the quicker the customer will get to know and trust you.

I need more time to consider your product. Sometimes more time, more discussions, and more people are needed. Sometimes the customer wants to be polite and delay the final decision or let you down easy by not directly saying no. The way to overcome this concern is to continue to work with your customer or work with a colleague of this customer to ensure that they see the value of your offer and truly want to purchase. When it is clear that they want to purchase, then you can work with them on what else needs to happen in order for them to move forward with you.

Is this your best price?

"Your price is too high." "I don't have the budget right now." I'd like to purchase your product but not at that price." "I always get a discount." The salesperson needs to work with his or her company to find the best offer that will beat inertia or the competition. The desired approach is to monetize the benefits for the customer so they see that the price is very low compared to the increase in revenue, savings in costs or time, and increase in their quality of life. The salesperson can try to add more value to the offer (additional services, terms, or conditions), work with his or her management to create an offer the customer cannot refuse or move on to the next opportunity. It is often safest to not comment on the prices of other companies. However, if the customer mentions a lower price alternative, one bold salesperson's response is: "Thank you for sharing their price, and I don't know why that company values its offering so low."

The following are the guidelines for creating win-win solutions in negotiations:

Plan and prepare: Decide ahead of time what your SMART (specific, measurable, actionable, realistic, time bound) goals—your maximum achievable and minimum acceptable goals. Prepare to ask questions, make your offer, answer objections, and follow-up so you best represent your company to each customer. Anticipate objections and prepare effective responses.

Communicate effectively: Honest dialogue in easy to understand language helps build trust and reduces customer anxiety and concern. When customers realize that they have their better interests in mind and when you are credible during the presentation, then their overall concern about the company and about you is reduced, and their confidence and trust in you is increased. When you don't know the answer to the question, let the customer know that you will find out. If you try to answer and are not correct or not clear, then the overall concern about you and the company is increased. Customers don't expect you to have all of the answers, and they expect you to follow-up and let them know the answer as soon as you can. When you say you will get the answer to them by a date or time, then you must deliver on that promise in order to earn their trust. If you make a commitment to the customer, then you must deliver on that commitment. Remember that when you make a commitment to the customer, it is a legal commitment that the company is bound to deliver (Johnston 2009, 209)

Stay positive: There is always a risk of becoming emotionally involved with the negotiations. Frustration, even anger, can be a part of the process. It is natural to try to defend yourself when you perceive you are being attacked. And, controlling your anger is critical. Stay calm, professional, and positive at all times. Ask questions to keep the customer involved and allow him or her to voice concerns because he or she may be frustrated or angry with the process also. Maintaining control demonstrates that you are committed to working with the customer to find a win–win solution.

Listen and Validate Customer Concerns

The salesperson can add value to the customer simply by listening carefully to and responding effectively to the customer's concerns. The selling process often requires that the customer takes a risk on something new. This potential change brings uncertainty and customers' need to know that you understand this and that you will be there to help the customer through this change.

Come Back to How You Help the Customer.

Remind the customer, as many times as appropriate, how you will help them and that your total offer that includes your product, your customer service, your attention to keeping the customer aware of advances in the field, your sharing of best practices with the customer, and all ways that you will help the customer be even more successful.

Objection Handling

There are nine common approaches to addressing customer's concerns. Effective salespeople can read the situation and use these approaches to help the customer continuing to move forward. These approaches are described in the following:

Question

You turn the customer's concern into a question and refocus on one or more strengths of your value proposition. You get the customer thinking in a new way and contrast his or her concern against an advantage that you offer. For example,

- Buyer: Your product is 10 percent more than that of your competitor!
- Seller: Yes, it is slightly more expensive, but do you agree that the higher quality means fewer returns and lower service costs for your company in the long run?

Direct Denial

You directly confront the information given. This is a confrontational strategy for dealing with customer objections. When you directly deny something a customer says, the customer may react negatively. So you use this strategy only when the customer states a clearly false and damaging statement about you, the company, or your product, and you deliver the message in a manner that is not offensive, insulting, or condescending.

- Buyer: I was told recently that you had to recall all of your production for the last two months because of a faulty relay in your switch mechanism.
- Seller: I'm not sure where you could have heard that. We have not had a recall on any of our products for over 10 years. If you like, I can provide the data for you. Your source was mistaken.

Indirect Denial

You begin by agreeing with the customer, validating the objection, and then explaining why it is untrue. This is softer than the direct denial.

- Buyer: Demand for your products is strong. I'm not convinced you will be able to meet my order on time.
- Seller: You are correct. My company has enjoyed tremendous success and we are thankful .... However, we pride ourselves on not missing order deadlines, and our customers will verify that ...

Compensating for Deficiencies

This approach moves the customer from focusing on a feature your product performs poorly to one in which it excels. You must be careful to pick a feature and benefit that is important to your customer.

- Buyer: The response time on your product is too slow. Your competition's response time is two-tenths of a second faster.
- Seller: I agree with you. My product is two-tenths of a second slower. However, please note that it also costs 25 percent less per unit ... and has 10 percent fewer returns ...

Feel Felt Found

You acknowledge the customer's feeling, extend the same feelings to a larger audience, and counter with a legitimate argument from the customers peers. Please note that this technique has been around for a long time, so you can use the spirit of the approach and add your words that reflect your true feelings and that make your comments genuine.

- Buyer: In my opinion, your products are overpriced and not worth the extra cost.
- Seller: Our products are slightly more that the competition's and I can certainly see why you *feel* that way. Other customers

have *felt* that way at first. However, when they take the time to examine the product quality, they have *found* the overall value to be worth the investment.

Third Party Endorsements

You use outside parties to endorse you or bolster your arguments in the presentation that adds credibility. This approach can be combined with other strategies.

- Buyer: Your customer service has been questionable, and it is important I have tech support 24/7.
- Seller: I agree with you that our customer service was not what it should be several years ago. However, we made the investment to improve customer service, and now it is among the best in the industry. Gracie Electronics felt as you did but was willing to try us and is now one of our best customers.

Bounce Back

This approach turns a customer's concern into a reason for action. This can be effective with objections about needing more time or wanting a lower price.

- Buyer: I've listened to your presentation but need more time to consider your proposal.
- Seller: I can appreciate that this is a big decision for your company. However, delaying this commitment only costs your company money. As we agreed earlier, my products will save nearly 40 percent ...

Defer

This can be used when the customer raises a concern about price early in the presentation, before the value proposition has been defined.

- Buyer: (before the full value of the product has been explained): What is the cost of your product?
- Seller: I can appreciate your interest in knowing the price of the product, but I would ask you to hold off just a minute until I know a little more about your product requirements …

Trial Offer

This approach lowers the risk to the customer and can calm customer's objections. You need to ensure that you clearly define the terms of the trial offer beforehand and that the customer is completely trained on how to use your product.

- Buyer: I'm not willing to make a commitment to your copier today. It seems complicated and hard to use.
- Seller: I can appreciate your concerns. How about I have our service department install one for you and let you try it for one week. I will come by and demonstrate it for you … (Johnston 2009, 211–15).

Sidebar:

Raving Fans

Raving fans describes customers who ….

purchase and believe in our products and people
are loyal and passionately recommend you to colleagues
provide unsolicited praise and suggestions to the company
will forgive poor quality and will tell you about them to help you
fix them
extol your virtues voluntarily to their colleagues and friends when
you are not there
feel connected to something bigger than themselves that your
company represents

Creating Raving Fans

Characteristics of a raving fan differ by company and market segment. The process of creating raving fans starts by defining characteristics of an ideal customer or *raving fan* by individual and institution. Once the ideal is defined, then the customer's status can be assessed, and specific actions can be created to bring the customer toward the raving fan goal. For example, a customer development plan can have three stages—beginner, intermediate, and advanced. The company can assess the status of the customer.

Using the following example (table below), the customer could be at *no plans for studies, publications, and speaking*, or Stage 1. The company and customer have conversations that result in clear definition of mutual goal to *do regional and national speaking*. Actions are then planned to achieve this goal, moving the customer from Stage 1 to Stage 3 for this criteria. A sample development assessment for physicians and nurses in a hospital setting is shown in the following.

Customer Development Assessment

	Stage 1 beginner	Stage 2 intermediate	Stage 3 advanced
Physicians	• Physicians somewhat interested	• One physician recognized as expert in the hospital, other physicians interested in therapy and product • Plan for studies, publications and speaking • Systematic fellows training on the therapy and product	• One strong physician leader, one or more fellow or attending leaders • Recognized as local or national leader in therapy • Leading physician speaking • Abstracts or posters or studies • Writing articles • Webinars • Protocol makes therapy safe, effective, and easy for physicians and nurses

Nurse leader-ship	• One leader • Train nurses on therapy and product with support • Address resistance to upgrading to the new product • Only using training tools from the company	• One leader recognized as therapy and product expert in the hospital • One super-user per department per shift • Planning to write, speak, or do studies • Require company's help two times per year or less to train nurse trainers • Interested in upgrading to the new system • Using superusers and hospital-specific tools to train • Periodically using run summaries from machines to assess and upgrade training • Departments collaborate to implement the therapy	• Reference source for testimonials—verbal or written—and on-site visits • Clear guidelines for use of therapy and products • One leader recognized as expert locally, regionally, or nationally • Two or more superusers per department per shift • Published or writing posters, abstracts, or articles • Speaking on therapy or product • Implementing studies • Participate in webinar or e-newsletter • Self-sufficient nurse training • Unit-based educators in each department • Reference source for testimonials—verbal or written—and on-site visits • A leader in using superusers and hospital-specific tools such as cards, e-mails, posters, laminated reminders • Systematically using run summaries from machines to upgrade training • Departments demonstrate excellent collaboration to improve the therapy

Success Factors for Great Sale People

What separates good from great salespeople? Great salespeople

1. Recognize and capitalize on opportunities to continually increase sales, profitability, and market share
2. Act as sales consultants making sound recommendations in a persuasive manner and create an environment of openness with customers. They understand the customers' industry and business and draw on many resources to add value to each customer.
3. Develop strategic partners by identifying potential businesses that can benefit from and contribute to a working relationship with his or her company and have the potential to become strategic partners with his or her company
4. Maintain strong business expertise by approaching their business form a consultant's perspective; understanding the business climate, economic indicators, market potential, and opportunities of their territory; and developing strong and effective resource networks (internal and external) and teams, use them effectively to bring exception value to customers, and anticipate obstacles, competitive solutions, and internal and external threats and then modify recommended solutions to be in a preferred situation.*

Summary

The product introduction team develops messaging, adapts the professional selling basics including the sales approach, negotiating techniques, and closing techniques to help the sales force be as effective as possible. The new product team also provides a roadmap for the sales team to follow to help develop customers and create raving fans. The following questions can help assess your readiness to launch:

1. How well do your messages persuade your target customers? What is working and what needs to be improved?

---

* Interview with Timothy J. Trow, Region Sales Manager, Tennant Company, San Antonio, Texas (Johnston 2009, 34).

2. Have you equipped the sales team with instructions and scripts that help them with the sales approach, negotiating and closing techniques?

3. Does your sales team have a clear roadmap to creating raving fans?

CHAPTER 5

Sales Training, Value Propositions, the Brand Promise, Pricing, Legal, and Ethical Considerations

It's a funny thing about life; if you refuse to accept anything but the best, you very often get it.

—W. Somerset Maugham

The quality of a person's life is in direct proportion to their commitment to excellence, regardless of their chosen field of endeavor.

—Vincent T. Lombardi

Don't be afraid to take a big step when one is indicated. You can't cross a chasm in two small steps.

—David Lloyd George

Introduction

The new product introduction team creates sales training, methods to enhance sales productivity, value propositions, the brand promise, and pricing. Throughout the process, the team needs to hold itself and all colleagues to high legal and ethical standards. This chapter discusses key issues in for each of these topics.

Sales Training

The pharmaceutical industry has traditionally hired people with limited sales experience and then systematically trains them in sales techniques, therapy, and product information. The training provides specific instructions on what to say to whom at what time. The sales professional is taught best practices and is tested on messages and objection handling until competent. In the field, sales managers work with the sales people to improve their skills. By contrast, traditional companies' hire experienced sales people with a successful sales track record. Other companies have sales training programs that are often less developed than pharmaceutical training programs. Still effective sales training needs to ensure compelling and consistent messages (what to ask, what to tell), sales tools that educate the customer, and competence in objection handling. The most effective product launches ensure that their sales team is trained in the products and selling approaches and competencies are validated in the classroom and in the field.

The selling process needs to be continually improved by testing new approaches that measurably improve pipeline value by stage, time to advance to the next stage, and time and success percentage of closing the opportunity. These measurements report productivity by sales person and groups to benchmark best performance that can lead to discovery and sharing of best practices across the sales team.

The most effective sales training programs include learning prior to a meeting, learning at a meeting, and follow-up learning in the field. Effective sales training programs use techniques that ensure that the

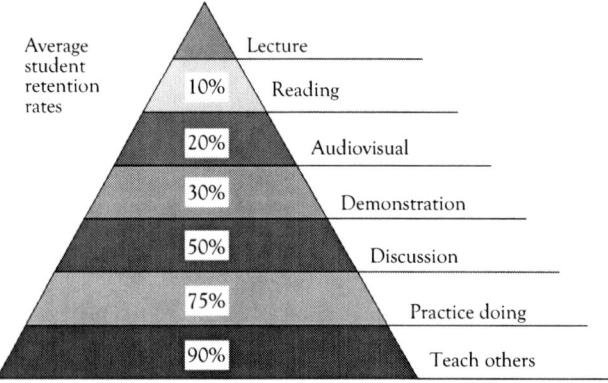

Figure 5.1 Learning pyramid

Source: National Training Laboratories, Bethel, Maine

learner becomes competent the topics that are required for performing the job. These techniques include lecture, reading, viewing videos, demonstrations, discussions, simulations, and having the learner teach others. Theoretical retention rates for each of these methods in shown in Figure 5.1. In addition, sales is learned on the job through trial and error and on joint sales calls with sales trainers, sales managers, marketing, research and development, and other colleagues.

Key Professional Selling Concepts

Effective sales people have a mindset that is ethical, expect success, and help customers be even more successful. At every sales training meeting, sales people need to be re-energized and motivated. Fundamental selling concepts that can be reviewed and provide motivation at any time include the following:

- Professional selling is helping
- Offer only something that you sincerely believe will serve the best interest of buyers
- What's In it For Me (WIIFM) …. Me means customer!
- Value = monetized benefits less costs
- Value elements: (1) increase revenue, (2) decrease time or cost, and (3) improve quality of life
- People buy on emotion and justify with facts
- Change model: (1) dissatisfied with today, (2) compelling vision of the future, and (3) easy steps to get there
- In sales and in the dictionary, No is just a word that comes before Yes. It may take nine messages before the customer will hear your message and say yes
- In sales, No means I need to kNow more about how you will make my life even better
- Three key questions:
  1. Can you see how this will help you _____ ?
  2. Are you seriously interested in _____?

3. Given your beliefs, when do you think it would be best to
   start _____?
- Objection handling: feel, felt, found, indirect denial, direct
  denial, compensating for deficiency

How Salespeople Spend Their Time

Salespeople do selling and nonselling activities. The selling activities
include preparing for, executing, and following up on customer interactions. The nonselling activities include administrative work such
as completing expense reports, putting information into a customer
relationship management system, coordinating delivery of products, and
working with colleagues on projects. One survey reported the following
breakdown of salesperson time:

Administrative tasks 34 percent
Waiting or travelling 32 percent
With customers 15 percent
Prospecting 14 percent
Service calls 5 percent

Companies need to continually improve how they help salespeople
spend more time in face-to-face contact or time in contact with customers and reduce the nonselling tasks as much as possible. The quality of
selling time is directly related to the salesperson's interaction with customers. In general, different modes of communication tend to enable
different results. For example, e-mail or text or Linkedin or Facebook
can build or maintain relationships. However, they can also unintention-
ally damage relationships because it is a one-way communication and the
reader assigns the emotion to the sender's words. The emotion assigned is
often negative or incorrect.

Phone can build relationships and can also effectively maintain relationships because it is a two-way communication that allows the caller
to hear tone of voice and adapt to the recipient. It is easier to say no
over the phone or break off the interaction, and the level of commitment

from each participant is lower so dealing with difficult issues can be more challenging.

Face-to-face communication is most effective at building relationships because it is the most complete two-way exchange between people. Face to face also shows the highest level of commitment from both parties so it predisposes the participants to collaborate. When we meet in person, we use words, tone of voice, and body language. We also perceive overall demeanor and appearance. This method allows the easiest give and take between two people. Our innate ability to size up the other person and decide to trust this person is completely engaged with face-to-face encounters. We make this assessment in the blink of an eye. FaceTime, Skype, and other video and audio communication tools lie between phone and face-to-face conversations.

Territory and Time Management

Professional sales people are paid to sell. In general, the more time they are face to face with customers, the more they sell. Tools that can help a sales person to be more efficient include the following:

- Effective training so the salesperson memorizes what is required and can quickly access what is required.
- Effective support from the home office, manager, and other colleagues so questions get answered quickly and the salesperson can keep moving the customer forward.
- Effective organization of key information related to making sales happen, including customer, product, and administrative information.
- Daily, weekly, and monthly planning so appointments are scheduled to maximize salesperson time in front of the customer and minimize travel time.
- Effective and efficient completion of required tasks for the home office such as expense reports, management reports, pipeline information, and requests for customer and competitive information.

Vignette

You Have Two Jobs; One of Them Is to Learn How to Do Your Job

Students getting ready to enter the world of business always ask about how long the training program is. *Forever* is not the answer they are looking for. Those who accept the fact that they have just been appointed director of training for themselves will go further and faster than any others. Learning the fact of the day is just the beginning. Finding out from customers what is going on in the trade so that pieces of the puzzle will begin to fit together is a never-ending project if you are to keep up with an ever-changing big picture. Technology moves. We all must move with it. Where it is going is always a good question to study. You don't have to lead the pack, but it's not a good thing to be deep in the second tier. You have to learn about general business and about world events, not because they will affect your business, but because well-rounded knowledge is apparent to those doing business with you. Trade data, technology developments, and world events are a big part of your training program. These are best learned every day rather than in formal programs. They require time and effort to be fit into a tight schedule. A ten-minute wait for an appointment can translate into two Wall Street Journal articles (if you have them in your bag). You are now attending *graduate school.* Study hard; it will pay off! (Falvey n.d.).

Value Propositions

The product introduction team creates detailed messages and objection handling for various levels in the organization (strategic, managerial, and operational) and for relevant constituents or departments (e.g., in the hospital market segment, this includes patients, physicians, nurses, administrators, biomedical engineers, and purchasing). Each customer will have different perceptions of the new product's value. The operational buyer has the shortest time horizon, so the relevant time period for assessing value may be one week or one month or one quarter. The managerial buyer will have a longer time horizon which could be one year or longer, and the strategic buyer could consider more variables, such as company reputation or synergy with other divisions, which an operational buyer would not consider.

Value to the health-care provider is the monetization of the product benefits that result in

1. Increasing revenue;
2. Decreasing costs or time; and
3. Improving quality of life of the patient and caregiver.

A product's value can be determined by clinical and market research as follows:

A product used by patients who are trained by nurses has the following benefits:

1. Easier to use; and
2. Less risk of infection.

The product value is the quantification of these benefits in terms of dollar.

1. Easier to use results in 30 minutes less training time and 10 percent less patient dropout from the procedure resulting in 12 more months for the patient on the therapy or $3,000 margin per year for the provider.
2. Less risk of infection results in $100 less per month in antibiotics, two fewer hospital days per year at $1,500 per day, and six more months on the therapy or $5,700 economic improvement for the health-care system.

Additional value beyond the product that can be monetized includes product reliability; consistent delivery; effective company resolution of issues; services provided by technical, sales, or clinical resources; reliability and quality of the product; and price.

Value may be thought of as a ration of benefits to costs. Customers invest in doing business with you, including financial, time, and effort to achieve a bundle of benefits from the company. The seller can increase the value of his or her offering by

- Raising the number or amount of benefits;
- Reducing the cost to the customer;
- Raising benefits and reducing costs;
- Raising benefits by more than the increase in costs; and
- Lowering the benefits by less than the reduction in costs.

For example, when we shop for a car, we add up and compare the costs and benefits for each alternative. We compare the total package that includes the price and bundle of benefits of each car and dealership.

The product introduction team needs to convincingly provide answers to the question "why buy from us now?" The most effective messaging includes questions, logical explanations, and facts that help the customer emotionally commit to the decision to change. An effective approach to changing customer behavior is to construct messages (what you ask and tell) that lead the customer to decide that they are dissatisfied with the present, desire the compelling vision of the future that you offer, and understand the easy steps to achieve the vision.

Case Study #1: Messaging

Situation

New technology has automatic measuring system instead of prior gold standard of scale measuring system. Feature: automatic measuring. Benefit: less nurse work. Value: 20 fewer tasks per shift for over 120 minutes saved so more time to care for the patient instead of running the machine.

Twenty second message: "Would you be interested in a system that gives you more time—two hours per shift—to care for your patient?"

Messaging

Ideally, you want your customer to assess your product and response with a heartfelt *WOW!* Products that evoke this response focus the customer on breakthrough advantages and customers are more likely to want to learn more about the product. The most powerful product introductions create conversations that enable the customer to quickly understand how the product will make his or her live better *and* enable the customer to powerfully articulate the value (quantified benefits) to their colleagues.

Follow-up Action

Continually test and refine messages to create effective 20-second, 2-minute, and 20-minute versions.

The Magic Question That Accelerates Sales

Many years ago, I worked for a company that provided IT systems integration services to large electronics manufacturers. Projects could run over $10 M so each deal was significant.

One night, I had dinner with the COO of a large potential customer. The COO's company was building a new factory. During dinner, I told the COO, "My company helped Motorola and Siemens use information technology to bring their new factory online six months ahead of schedule. Their faster time-to-production enabled them to generate hundreds of millions in incremental profits. Then I asked, "Would you like to learn more about what they did?"

He put down his fork and quickly answered yes. This one question opened the door to a very large order.

Over the years, I've learned that initiating the sales process by asking a single attention-grabbing, curiosity-raising question is the most effective way to accelerate revenues.

The Magic Question™ is that one question you need to ask to get the prospect to say "please tell me more." The trick is to generate curiosity quickly.

A typical Magic Question starts with a short story of the form "My company has developed (a new product) that has helped (a leading company in the customer's industry) achieve (the following important business benefits). It then goes in for the (sales) kill by asking, "Would you like to learn how we did it?" If phrased properly, the prospect can't help but say yes. You have now grabbed their attention and gained their implicit permission to continue to ask more exploratory questions.

While the concept of The Magic Question seems simple, developing effective Magic Questions requires close cooperation between *sales* and *marketing*. It is marketing's responsibility to drive creation of The Magic Question. Marketing must provide the following:

- clear description of what you want sales to sell;
- References that are respected by your prospect; and
- Concisely stated business benefits delivered by your solution that you know will resonate with your prospects.

Is your sales force prepared with the training and tools to drive the conversation further and accelerate the sales cycle if the prospect answers, "yes, tell me more?" Or must your sales team wait for the corporate cavalry to arrive to continue the dialogue? Forcing a delay by improperly equipping sales will unnecessarily slow the sales cycle. As many sales executives have told me, "delays have killed many deals," it is marketing's responsibility to ensure that sales is equipped to use The Magic Question to accelerate closing business.

The process of generating The Magic Question can be a powerful test of your understanding of the business value delivered by your product.

Do you know The Magic Question for each of your product and services? (Baron 2010)

The Brand Promise

The brand promise is the commitment from made from the company and brand to the customer. The brand promise is often one sentence, and can be developed based on the features, functional advantages, emotional rewards, values of the target customers and personality of the brand. The brand promise conveys the feeling that the company wants its customers to feel. The 3M brand promise pyramid in Figure 5.2 shows the elements of a brand promise.

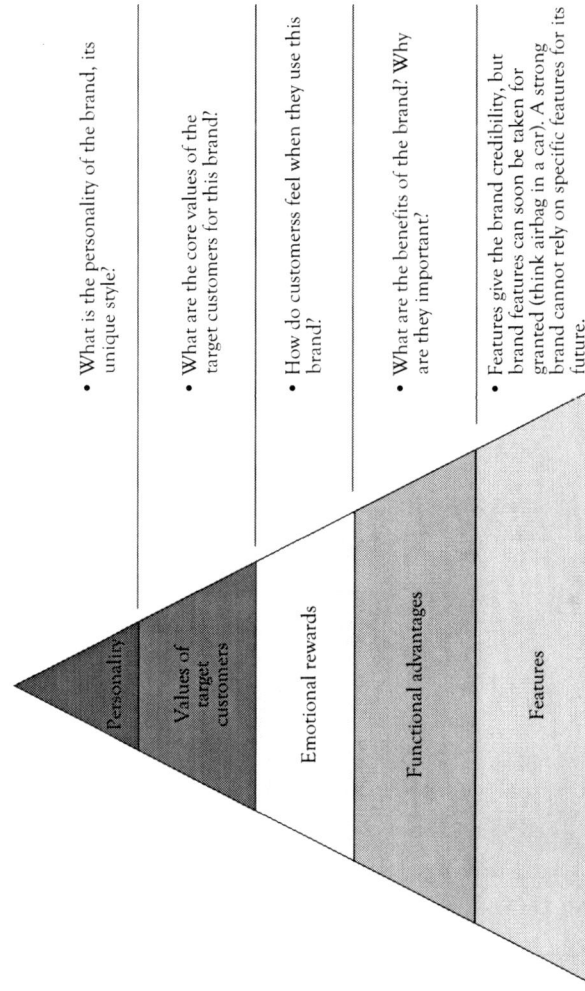

- What is the personality of the brand, its unique style?

- What are the core values of the target customers for this brand?

- How do customerss feel when they use this brand?

- What are the benefits of the brand? Why are they important?

- Features give the brand credibility, but brand features can soon be taken for granted (think airbag in a car). A strong brand cannot rely on specific features for its future.

Figure 5.2 The brand promise

Source: http://marketminute.typepad.com/photos/uncategorized/brand_promise.jpg

Brand promises from three highly successful, world-wide brands are listed as follows:

> *The NFL*: "To be the premier sports and entertainment brand that brings people together, connecting them socially and emotionally like no other."
>
> *Coca-Cola*: "To inspire moments of optimism and uplift."
>
> *Virgin*: "To be genuine, fun, contemporary, and different in everything we do at a reasonable price."

The Promise

The most powerful value proposition includes a specific, monetized promise to the customer. One format for creating promise that is tailored to the specific needs of the customer is shown as follows:

Our promise to you:

Starting on	(put date here)
Because you are using	(put your company and product here)
You will attain	(put the expected results)
By	(date by which results will be attained)
As measured by	(measurement methodology)

This promise can be strengthened by including the specific objectives and shared risk and reward into the legal agreement with the customer. For example, a company can promise to reduce hospitalizations by 10 days per month (let's assume $1,000 in variable costs to the hospital per day) due to use of its product, and the agreement can state that for every reduced hospital day, the hospital benefit is $1,000 variable cost per day and that the company will receive 20 percent of the savings or $200 per day, or that the price of the product will increase the following year to capture a portion of the savings delivered to the hospital.

Great brands have four characteristics. The brand is

1. Unique, for example, Ikea furniture has exclusive, on-trend styling at unbelievable prices.
2. Consistent, for example, Red Bull looks and tastes the same no matter where you buy it.
3. Relevant, for example, Mini Cooper looks cool and doesn't use much gas, and you can design you own online.
4. Emotionally connecting, for example, an iPad, with hundreds of personalized qualities, becomes a loved companion (Richmond 2010, 15).

The ideal brand has these characteristics that predispose the customer to view the brand favorably and transfer the positive, trusted feelings of the brand to the salesperson.

Voice of the Customer

The introduction team analyzes the *voice of the customer*, or *the collective insight into customer needs, wants, perceptions, and preferences gained through direct and indirect questioning* and observation. "These discoveries are translated into meaningful company actions objectives that help."[*]
The company increases value delivered to the customer and captures a portion of this created value for the company's shareholders.

The insights that are most important come from the most valuable and most growable customers. These insights need to be sought after in a systematic manner. Topics to probe and monitor include actual value delivered (compared to the competition and the status quo), product and company awareness, brand preference and impact on purchase decision, message effectiveness, pricing, buying preferences, buying behaviors, benchmarking with competition, and expected competitive responses.

One crucial component of the *voice of the customer* is providing ongoing, thoughtful, honest advice from individuals in the company's high-value target segment. These individuals are in an ongoing conversation about all elements of the product and company. These customers coach and

---

[*] See businessdictionary.com

advise the company on how it goes to market and how it can more effectively and quickly create raving fans.

These customer advisors provide input on product development ideas, messages on improved clinical outcomes and lower total costs, pricing, competitive positioning, and future product and service needs. All elements of the product introduction are discussed. Proof statements can be well-designed studies, observational studies, case studies, registry or collection of data, publications, presentations, posters, abstracts, white papers, editorials, testimonials. The goal for each of these advisors is to have their institution become a reference center. After reference advisors and institutions are in place, then the company needs to take actions to connect the reference center to other target institutions via e-mail, phone, webinars, visits to the reference center site, and visits for the advisor or expert to other sites. Each individual reference needs to have sufficient experience with the product and interaction with the company to ensure that they have high-quality insights and are well-informed perspective on all relevant aspects of the product and company. This deep understanding of the product, coupled with the reference's clinical experience and knowledge of peer practices, enables high-quality input to major decisions concerning the product introduction. The best portfolio of references includes well-known, influential clinicians and administrators who are in demand for their expertise, and who share their perspectives regularly, and references from each target segment for the product (e.g., academic and nonacademic institutions, and geographic mix) as well as leading customers who have the highest usage levels can influence other high-volume users to join your company.

It is important to capture and be able to measure and track patient satisfaction. The net promoter score is a useful tool to get the overall impression of the customer experience. Combining the net promoter score with a few additional questions can be an effective approach to gathering and monitoring the customer experience.

The net promoter score question is

How likely are you to recommend this product to a friend? 0 = not at all likely, 10 = Extremely likely

Customers can be categorized as follows:

=*Promoters* (score 9 to 10) are loyal enthusiasts who will keep buying and refer others, fueling growth.

=*Passives* (score 7 to 8) are satisfied but unenthusiastic customers who are vulnerable to competitive offerings.

=*Detractors* (score 0 to 6) are unhappy customers who can damage your brand and impede growth through negative word-of-mouth.

To calculate your company's net promoter score, take the percentage of customers who are promoters and subtract the percentage of customers who are detractors.*

Additional questions to add to the net promoter question to gather meaningful insights are

- Why did you select this score?
- What did you like best about your experience?
- What would you like to see improved?

Examples of voice of the customer methods.

Case Study #2: Consulting Group

Description

A group of 50 physicians, 25 from large academic centers and 25 from private centers (a representative mix of the market), met annually. The agenda included the most important topics in the therapy and related to the company's future plans.

Actions

Annual meetings and year-long working groups (with meetings at professional conferences, phone, and e-mail) on key topics (infections, quality improvement, dosing, technology).

---

* http://www.netpromoter.com/why-net-promoter/know/

Value to the Company

Significantly higher than average therapy usage (24 percent vs. 17 percent country average) and market share (96 percent vs. 71 percent market average) among the consulting group. Unsolicited word-of-mouth promotion from this group to their colleagues. Orchestrated interactions that enable this group to share their enthusiasm and experience with colleagues. Improved company new products, messages, and marketing plans.

Value to the Consultants

Connection with thought leaders. Keep current on the latest breaking therapy and product information. Directed company to better serve customers. Insights from conversation during informal discussions.

Case Study #3: Customer Strategic Planning Group

Description

Six physicians met two times in 12 months. The agenda included improvements needed from the medical device companies and discussion of all companies in the market.

Actions

Two face-to-face group meetings, several individual meetings, and phone calls in between the meetings.

Value to the Company

Specific ideas on how to improve messages, pricing, and the product. More detailed and powerful value (quantified benefits) messages and consultative selling approach.

Value to Participants

Systematic input on how to improve the company. Develop relationships and exchange information with colleagues.

Case Study #4: Scientific Advisory Board

Description

Seven physicians from well-known hospitals. The same physicians meet for 1.5 days each six months. In addition to the formal meetings, there are conference calls, calls, and e-mails during the year.

Value to the Company

Honest feedback over time on plans and implemented product improvements, messages, and programs. Relationships that ensure unfiltered, clear, and transparent idea exchange.

Value to the Advisor

Continual positive influence to improve the company and medical community. Idea exchange with company experts and colleagues.

Case study #5: Customer Input—Observation

Description

Observation: Company personnel observes customers performing the function to identify unmet needs

Surveys: Online, face-to-face interview, phone, and paper or fax format to gather information.

Focus groups: Bring multiple customers together for a moderated session

Conversations: Face-to-face, phone, and e-mail conversations with customers who are interested in ongoing dialogue with the company.

The product introduction team sets up communication vehicles (group e-mails, phone groups, conference calls, internal blogs, other) so that all affected people can stay current with the latest information and offer ideas to help the product introduction. These communication vehicles need to be thoughtfully created and include people at the appropriate time. For example, senior managers may get detailed weekly updates and the sales team may get more general information. The product introduction team could have a few sales leaders and managers who help distill the relevant information to be shared with the entire sales team. The rationale for carefully sharing information with the sales team is to ensure that they are informed on what they need to know and are not distracted from their short-term goals.

Legal and Ethical Considerations for Sales Professionals

Our society sets legal standards for behavior of buyers and sellers. The Uniform Commercial Code (UCC) consists of nine articles and declares rules and procedures for business practices in the United States. Article 2 is titled "Sales" and it defines terms and legal obligations for buyers and sellers.

The salesperson has significant legal responsibilities, including

1. Representing the company. Since a salesperson is a legal representative of the company, his or her words carry a legal obligation for their employer. Quite simply, salespersons are speaking for the entire company when they are in front of the customer. Any statement, promise, or action is technically a statement from the company and is a legal commitment.

2. Oral versus written commitments. The UCC considers an oral commitment from a salesperson legally binding to the company. Any sale over $500 does require a written agreement; however, salespeople need to know that statements made in front of the customer carry just as much weight as a written contract.

3. Implied and express warranties. Products and services often come with express warranties that assure the buyer that the product will perform as represented by the company. However, salespeople need to be careful because statements they make regarding product and service performance, even if they are not consistent with company materials, can constitute an implied warranty. This is especially important in relationship selling. If the salesperson, after learning about the customers' needs, presents the product as a solution, there is an implied warranty the product will do the job.

Unlawful business activities are defined in the Sherman Antitrust Act, Clayton Act, and Robinson–Patman Act. State and municipalities have statutes and can pass laws that directly affect selling. For example, every state has its own set of real estate laws, which influence the sale of real estate in that state. The following are some unlawful activities:

- Collusion: when companies get together to fix prices or unfairly bias a selling process.
- Restraint of trade: force a dealer to stop carrying a competitors' product
- Competitor obstruction: impeding a competitor's access to a customer
- Competitor defamation: harm a competitor by making unfair or untrue statements about the company, products, or employees. Defamation can be slander or libel. Slander is unfair or untrue oral statements. Libel is unfair or untrue written statements that materially harm the reputation of the competitor or the personal reputation of an employee.
- Price discrimination: giving different prices to different customers who purchase the same quality and quantity of the product or service. Companies are allowed to charge different prices if they (1) reflect differences in the cost of operations (manufacturing, sales, or delivery), (2) meet competitor pricing to the same customers, or (3) reflect differences in the quality or quantity of the product purchase. It is legal to charge a lower price to a customer who buys more or has received a better price from a competitor. At the end of the day, the issue is the fair treatment of customers (Johnston 2010, 119).

Business ethics define principles that define right and wrong and guide behavior in business. Companies need to define a code of conduct that describes acceptable and unacceptable behaviors related to their business. The code of conduct needs to address honesty, integrity, confidentiality, use of confidential information, gifts, and relationships with employees and customers and other topics that define behaviors of an ethical professional salesperson.

Dell Computer has a code of conduct for their company, not just for their salespeople, that sets expectations for behavior, including ethical issues, with the goal of making employees, customers, and stakeholders understand that they can "believe what we say and trust what we do." The following are the standards of ethical behaviors.

- Trust: Our word is good. We keep our commitments to each other and to our stakeholders.
- Integrity: We do the right thing without compromise. We avoid even the appearance of impropriety.
- Honest: What we say is true and forthcoming, not just technically correct. We are open and transparent in our communications with each other and about business performance.
- Judgment: We think before we act and consider the consequences of our action.
- Respect: We treat people with dignity and value their contributions. We maintain fairness in all relationships.
- Courage: We speak up for what is right. We report wrongdoing when we see it.
- Responsibility: We accept the consequences of our actions. We admit our mistakes and quickly correct them. We do not retaliate against those who report violations of law or policy.

The Direct Selling Association has published their ethical standards since the 1970s. Their 2011 version of the Standards that Ethical Independent Salespersons Should Follow (*Posted on 24 October 2011,* from the Direct Selling Association) is listed in the following.

The Standards that Ethical Independent Salespersons Should Follow are

- Offers should be clear, so that consumers may know exactly what is being offered and the extent of the commitment they are considering.

- A description of the goods and quantity purchased, and the price and terms of payment should be clearly stated on the order form together with any additional charges.
- Contracts or receipts use should conform to applicable laws or regulations.
- Any guarantee or warranty stated by the sales representative should be consistent with, and at least as protective as, that of the manufacturer or supplier of the product sold.
- Any description of after-sale service should be accurate and clear.
- Any receipt or contract copy should show the name of the sales representative and his or her address or the name, address, and telephone number of the firm whose product is sold.
- All salespersons should immediately identify themselves to a prospective customer and should truthfully indicate the purpose of their approach to the consumer, identifying the company or product brands represented.
- Salespersons should not create confusion in the mind of the consumer, abuse the trust of the consumer, or exploit the lack of experience or knowledge of the consumer.
- A salesperson should not imply that a prospective customer has been *specially selected* to receive some reputed benefit or that any offer is special or limited as to time when such is not the case.
- Salespersons should respect the privacy of the consumers by making every effort to make calls at a time that will suit their convenience and wishes. Selling contacts should not be intrusive and the right of the consumer to terminate sales interview should be scrupulously respected.
- All references to testimonials and endorsements should be truthful, currently applicable, and authorized by the person or organization giving same.
- If product comparisons are made, they should be fair and based on facts that have been substantiated.

- A salesperson should refrain for disparagement of other products or firms.
- A salesperson should not attempt to induce the consumer to cancel a contract he or she has made with another salesperson.*

Another version of a code of ethics was created by Steven L. Boyle and is described in his blog post as follows:

A Code of Ethics for Salespeople to Live By—It is Time to Change Society's Perception of "Sales People" by Steven L. Boyle

It is time to get people to *trust* the sales profession again. Through all of the downed economies and the recessions of the past, one career has always survived, *sales*.

Now over the years, a lot of people's perceptions of salespeople were spoiled by one rotten apple in the bunch, and in all fairness, that is all it takes. Today I say stand tall, be proud of your profession and realize we are the highest paid profession out there, if you are good at it. No one is just good at being a Doctor or a Lawyer, they studied hard, earned certifications, and crafted their art over years of practice, but most importantly they live by a code of ethics.

Here are mine …. Feel free to make them yours, and let's start something bigger than any of us. Let's change the perception of salespeople for future generations to come.

I will

1. Maintain honesty and integrity in all relationships with customers, prospective customers, and colleagues and continually work to earn their trust and respect.
2. Accurately represent my products or services to the best of my ability in a manner that places my customer or prospective customer and my company in a position that benefits both.
3. Respect and protect the proprietary and confidential information entrusted to me by my company and my customers and not engage in activities that may conflict with the best interest of my customers or my company.

---

* http://ethics.iit.edu/ecodes/node/3058

4. Continually upgrade my knowledge of my products or services, skills, and industry.

5. Use the time and resources available to me only for legitimate business purposes. I will only participate in activities that are ethical and legal, and when in doubt, I will seek counsel.

6. Respect my competitors and their products and services by representing them in a manner which is honest, truthful, and based on accurate information that has been substantiated.

7. Endeavour to engage in business and selling practices that contribute to a positive relationship with the community.

8. Assist and counsel my fellow sales professionals where possible in the performance of their duties.

9. Abide by and encourage others to adhere to this *code of ethics*.

As a certified sales professional, I understand that the reputation and professionalism of all salespeople depends on me as well as others engaged in the sales profession, and I will adhere to these standards to strengthen the reputation and integrity for which we will strive.*

The Sale and Marketing Executives International (SMEI) is an organization dedicated to ethical standards, continuing professional development, knowledge sharing, mentoring students, and advancing free enterprise. As no other worldwide executive sales and marketing associations exist, SMEI fills a void by providing a personal and professional community devoted to providing knowledge, growth, leadership, and connections between peers in both sales and marketing. SMEI has developed a Sales and Marketing Creed that states standards for sales and marketing executives.

Sales and Marketing Creed: The International Code of Ethics for Sales and Marketing

Your pledge of high standards in serving your company, its customers, and free enterprise

---

* http://consultativesalescanada.blogspot.com/2009/10/code-of-ethics-for-salespeople-to-live.html (Thursday, October 22, 2009).

- *I hereby acknowledge* my accountability to the organization for which I work and to society as a whole to improve sales' knowledge and practice and to adhere to the highest professional standards in my work and personal relationships.
- *My concept of selling* includes as its basic principle the sovereignty of all consumers in the marketplace and the necessity for mutual benefit to both buyer and seller in all transactions.
- *I shall personally maintain* the highest standards of ethical and professional conduct in all my business relationships with customers, suppliers, colleagues, competitors, governmental agencies, and the public.
- *I pledge to protect*, support, and promote the principles of consumer choice, competition, and innovation enterprise, consistent with relevant legislative public policy standards.
- *I shall not knowingly participate* in actions, agreements, or marketing policies or practices that may be detrimental to customers, competitors, or established community social or economic policies or standards.
- *I shall strive to ensure* that products and services are distributed through such channels and by such methods as will tend to optimize the distributive process by offering maximum customer value and service at minimum cost while providing fair and equitable compensation for all parties.
- *I shall support efforts* to increase productivity or reduce costs of production or marketing through standardization or other methods, provided these methods do not stifle innovation or creativity.
- *I believe prices* should reflect true value in use of the product or service to the customer, including the pricing of goods and services transferred among operating organizations worldwide.
- *I acknowledge* that providing the best economic and social product value consistent with cost also includes (a) recognizing the customer's right to expect safe products with clear instructions for their proper use and maintenance; (b) providing

easily accessible channels for customer complaints; (c) investigating any customer dissatisfaction objectively and taking prompt and appropriate remedial action; (d) recognizing and supporting proven public policy objectives such as conserving energy and protecting the environment.

- *I pledge my efforts* to assure that all marketing researches, advertisements, and presentations of products, services, or concepts are done clearly, truthfully, and in good taste so as not to mislead or offend customers. I further pledge to assure that all these activities are conducted in accordance with the highest standards of each profession and generally accepted principles of fair competition.
- *I pledge to cooperate* fully in furthering the efforts of all institutions, media, professional associations, and other organizations to publicize this creed as widely as possible throughout the world.*

Customer Relationship (or Experience) Management

Definition and Goals of Customer Relationship Management

Customer relationship management (CRM) is a philosophy that uses computer software to collect and use customer's information to get, keep, and grow profitable customers. The CRM philosophy sees every interaction between your company and the customer as an opportunity to grow the business relationship. The philosophy develops trust, concentrates company efforts on high-value customers, and changes the company to better service the most valuable and most growable customers. High-value customers are those that deliver the highest lifetime value to the company. The philosophy enables the salesperson to know about all important interactions with the customer so that he or she can continually build the relationship as opposed to not knowing

---

* Sales & Marketing Executives International, Inc., http://www.smei.org/displaycommon.cfm?an=1&subarticlenbr=16

all relevant information and needing to ask the customer for baseline information that is not moving the relationship forward can crowds out time to more completely understand the customers' needs and satisfy them.

The software provides structure and storage of relevant information such as customer purchases, service records, contact details, and insights that help the salesperson and company better serve the customer. The software collects data on customers so the company can perform analysis that will reveal traits associated with the most and least valuable customers. The software can also provide sales pipeline information that enables the sales representative and sales management clear and transparent visibility to the probability and size of the sales pipeline.

Organizations need to get, keep, and grow profitable customers. Customer relationship management supports this goal because better customer relationships can lead to better competitive success.

> If you are my customer and I get you to talk to me, and I remember what you tell me, then I get smarter and smarter about you until I know something about you my competitors don't know. So I can do things for you may competitors can't do, because they don't know you as well as I do. Before long, you can get something from me you can't get anywhere else, for any price. At the very least, you'd have to start all over somewhere else, but starting over is more costly than staying with me, so long as you like me and trust me to look out for your best interests. (Peppers 2011, 11)

The IDIC model provides a powerful framework to construct and improve the customer relationship management program:

- *Identify* your customer by relevant pieces of information so that you recognize the person and their up-to-date situation at every contact.
- *Differentiate* customers by creating groups based on value to the customer and customer's needs.

- *Interact* with them in ways that improve cost efficiency and the effectiveness of your interaction
- *Customize* some aspect of the products or services you offer; treat customer differently based on your interactions (adapted from Peppers 2011)

Promotion

The promotion plan details how the company will connect with the target audience. Communication vehicles include the sales force, press releases, newspaper, radio, TV, journals, magazines, investors, websites, e-mails, webinars, podcasts, white papers, facility tours, peer events for people who buy the product and people who influence the buying process, social media (Facebook, blogs, twitter, etc.), and so on. Each communication vehicle requires its own messages and message frequency tailored to the target group and communication vehicle. For example, a journal article could describe a well-designed clinical and economic study with significant scientific content published one time, press releases could be shorter and briefly announce important advances on a monthly basis, or webinars could share important information from case studies on a quarterly basis. Today, there is more opportunity for dialogue with customers and companies need to construct a promotion or feedback plan that takes advantage of this capability to increase two-way and continual communications and connection with customers and prospects. Companies can keep their messages "fresh by tying the launch into the larger business or technology issues the product serves ... the more you wrap around the through its launch period and beyond," the longer and louder your message will last.*

---

* *Alan E. Gold, the Chief Marketing Officer at TradeStone Software, Inc.* E-mail: agold@tradestonesoftware.com *See* http://www.linkedin.com/news?viewArticle=&articleID=177524470&gid=37751&type=member&item=27816631&articleURL=http%3A%2F%2Fwww%2Egreenbuzzagency%2Ecom%2Feight-rules-for-marketing-anewproduct&urlhash=yuZn&goback=%2Egde_37751_member_27816631

Pricing

The price of the product, and how company representatives talk about the price strongly influences the customer's perception of the company. Pricing decisions are informed by analysis of the voice of the customer, competition, expected customer response, expected competitor response, and nonprice elements such as payment terms, warranty, and in-depth understanding of the value of the product. In order to determine the value of the new product, the company needs to quantify the impact of the new product's benefits compared to the status quo and competition.

For example, assume that a new feature enable the new product to deliver the benefit of *saving nurse time.* The value of this benefit could be *one minute per week* or *four hours per day.* Let's assume that a nurse is paid $50.00 per hour. The quantification of the benefit, or value, of this product would range from pennies per week to $200.00 per day. The company, based on facts, needs to declare an expected value as well as provide worksheets and the method to confirm this value over time based on customer's data or perception. The most successful new products clearly show superior economic performance compared to the status quo and competitive products. An example graph is shown in Figure 5.3.

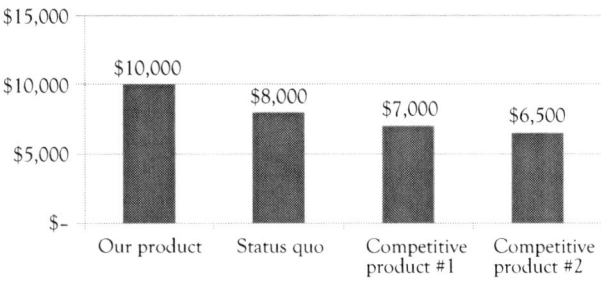

Figure 5.3 Profit comparison by product

Case Study #6: Pricing

Situation

Company with no track record in the market niche prices system 30 percent below existing products. This was needed to provide a compelling reason for hospitals to take the risk and purchase from this new company. This pricing provided acceptable gross margins for the company because their product costs were lower than the competition. Minimal discounts for large volume purchasers.

Actions

1. Quantification of the value of the system to the hospital, including equipment costs, maintenance and repairs, disposable pricing, and usage frequency, revealed that the new product delivered even more value to the hospitals than originally believed at the time of the introduction
2. Quality of the product improved some (not dramatically) over three years
3. Raised the floor prices to all customers and tiered pricing for lower prices for higher volume customers where the competition was most fierce
4. Anticipated and experienced competitor offering steep discounts in high-value customers

Result

1. Incremental revenue and gross margin increase by 10 percent
2. No negative impact on market share or customer satisfaction (sensitive cases were handled with care)
3. Tiered pricing motivated 10 percent additional purchases in many hospitals
4. Price reductions in high-value hospitals matched competitors aggressive discounts and the company won the business

Case Study #3: Pricing: Ultrabag 1992

Situation

Company was market leader with 70 percent market share in this market segment. Unmet need was to reduce patient's infection rate. New product with early data showing 50 percent reduction in infection rates and easier for patients to use. Division president selected to maximize price in the early adopter segment. The President of the United States wanted to get "all the short-term value we can since new product launches are infrequent." This niche strategy had 25 percent premium price and counted on

1. Price insensitive customers would purchase (approximately 10 percent of the market); and
2. Manufacturing costs were unable to be reduced quickly and were estimated to be nearly all of the price premium due to increased labor and low volumes due to ramp up, sterilization, and distribution costs, so there is no gross margin improvement.

Some customers purchased the product and only used it on the patients with the most infection risk. Those who purchased and who chose to not purchased were outraged by the high price. They perceived the product to be significantly better, and they saw the price increase as *gouging* and an unwise idea that limited their access to the product. This significantly reduced customer satisfaction whether customers purchased or not.

Actions

Market feedback was continuously analyzed. After many real-time updates, and two months of systematic review, the company switched from the niche strategy to a strategy to convert all patients to this product. This plan counted on

1. Switching competitive business for market share gain and cannibalizing existing products for therapy improvement, customer satisfaction, and customer retention, and

2. Fast reduction in manufacturing costs to below existing products. The global division president, company president, and CEO worked with manufacturing to reduce the costs at increased volumes and elimination of 50 SKUs of products to be cannibalized so gross margins would be increased with the new product.

Value of Niche Strategy

Quantitative

- $3,500 price increase per patient per year × 10 percent of patients × 15,000 patients = $5,250,000
- no gross margin improvement because manufacturing states higher standard costs at $3,500 per year

Qualitative

- High dissatisfaction from existing customers who purchase and who chose to not purchase due to price.
- Limited number of patients receive the product so few patients benefit.
- Few competitive conversions due to high price.
- No manufacturing efficiencies due to the relatively low volume of the new product.

Value of Full Conversion Strategy

Quantitative

- $350 price increase per patient per year × 100% × 15,000   = $5,250,000
- Gross margin improvement: $200/ patient/year × 15,000   = $3,000,000

- Competitive conversions: 2.5% market
  share = 500 patients × $23,000   = $1,500,000

  | | Total Year 1 | = $9,750,000 |

Qualitative

- Customers were thrilled to be able to offer the improved therapy to all patients.
- Customers were willing to switch patients to try the new product for a modest price increase.
- Due to high volume, manufacturing efficiencies reduced costs to below existing products and low-volume product codes were eliminated resulting in savings by reduction in unproductive production line changes and reduction in purchases of low-volume material changes.

Results

Clinical results were proven in post marketing studies. From the customer perspective, the value was calculated based on customer assumptions. The price settled at a 4-percent increase, and over 24 months, market share grew by 9 percent to 79 percent. This was considered a huge success!

Place (Distribution)

The product introduction team plans how the product will be delivered to the market. An analysis of profitability and strategic alignment clarifies which channel or channels create the most company value.

Distribution channels for products can be direct from the company to the customer through the sales team, through independent sales representatives, through distributors or resellers who have relationships with or a focus on the target markets, and online.

This analysis needs to compare the following factors for each distribution channel and for each potential partner in that channel:

- Strategic fit—how will this affect target customer perception of your product and company? If a partner has other products, how will the customer perceive the addition of your product? What is the track record and reputation of the partner in your target market? Does the partner have long-term relationships with your target market?
- Timing of revenue and profit streams—some partners can start up quickly, some will take more time. When do you break even on your costs of starting up with the partner and net positive cash flow?
- Timing of launching your product with the partner—will the partner be able to devote the time, resources, and effort to make your product launch successful? Are there other product launches or issues with other company's product lines that could reduce the commitment to your product?
- Ease and cost of training the partner—who needs to be trained and what do they need to know?
- Ease of supporting the partner—will the working relationship be relatively smooth or turbulent?
- Contract considerations—can you work out contract terms, minimum quantities, and other items to mutual satisfaction of you and the partner?
- Exit strategy—if new and more attractive partners appear, can you take advantage of them, given your existing partner relationships?

Go-to-Market Plan

A go-to-market plan for a new product describes the market landscape and key actions that will make the company optimize the product launch. This plan describes the vision for the new product, the competitive landscape, and the marketing and sales plans and describes how each function will contribute to the launch and a one-page summary.

Summary

The new product introduction team can ask the following questions:

1. Does the sales training program meet the needs of the sales team?
2. What methods have you developed to enhance sales productivity?
3. How powerful are your value propositions? How do your customers react to them?
4. Do customers clearly understand why they need to buy from you now? Are the reasons to buy compelling enough so that customers make commitments to you? Why or why not?
5. Is your brand promise tailored to the specific situation and economics of each customer?
6. Does your pricing achieve its objectives? How could you change your pricing and be even more successful?
7. Are your colleagues aware of and adhere, to your company's ethical and legal standards?

CHAPTER 6

New Product Launch Checklist

Security is mostly a superstition. It does not exist in nature …. Life is either a daring adventure, or nothing.

—Helen Keller

One does not discover new lands without consenting to lose sight of the shore for a very long time.

—Andre Gide

Enthusiasm is the electricity of life. How do you get it? You act enthusiastic until you make it a habit. Enthusiasm is natural; it is being alive, taking the initiative, seeing the importance of what you do, giving it dignity and making what you do important to yourself and others.

—Gordon Parks

There are no speed limits on the road to excellence.

—David W. Johnson

Introduction

The new product checklist was created from the review of best practices. This checklist is a convenient and systematic method to ensure that you have followed, or at least considered, proven best practices for new product launches.

New Product Launch Checklist

The new product launch checklist will increase the probability of success of the product introduction and the value it provides to the market and company. Companies can tailor this document to suit their specific market, company, and competitive situation to optimize the value to their customers and shareholders. Companies can continually improve their checklist by revising it based on input from advisors and input from customers and by debriefing after the introduction of each product. The checklist unique to each company can become the repository for institutional knowledge that provides competitive advantage and ensures that the company learns from its mistakes and captures best practices from other companies.

"When we look closely, we recognize the same balls being dropped over and over, even by those of great ability and determination .We know the patterns. We see the costs. It's time to try something else. Try a checklist." (Gawande 2010)

The product introduction checklist can ensure that key decisions are appropriately considered. This checklist can be tailored to each organization by getting input from key leaders and customers who can add, delete, and modify the items.

The New Product Launch Checklist

Leadership and Management

- ☐ Product introduction team's success factors
  - ☐ Defined team structure: team leader, teammates, meeting frequency (face to face, phone, electronic), reporting system to senior management, and stakeholders
  - ☐ All relevant functions are represented
  - ☐ Clear, transparent, and documented rules for effective communication with colleagues on and outside the team, including action plans with who does what by when
  - ☐ Decision-making rules are clear, transparent, and documented
  - ☐ Define and only accept a winning attitude from everyone working on the project
  - ☐ One-page document analyzing the effectiveness of key change variables: vision, SMART (specific, measurable, actionable, realistic, time bound) goals, strategy, required resources, skills, and actions. Assess strengths, weaknesses, and gaps.
  - ☐ Define product purpose, such as *dramatically improve clinical outcomes and lower total costs*
  - ☐ Communication vehicles (group e-mail, blog, phone groups, other) to all affected colleagues (at the appropriate time, e.g., a company may not want to distract the entire sales force, choosing to work closely with a smaller group such as two sales people, one sales director, and one vice president of sales)
- ☐ Clear monitoring system for the Food and Drug Administration (FDA) approval process to anticipate questions and revise estimate product approval to market
- ☐ Financial planning
  - ☐ Develop revenue, gross profit, and EBIT (earnings before interest and taxes) projections compared with monthly results, and calculate the impact on company valuation

- o Ensure that forecasts are provided to all departments (manufacturing, marketing, sales, customer service, etc.) with adequate time to create realistic plans
- ☐ Preparation completed by department: marketing, sales, manufacturing, distribution, customer service, clinical education, finance, technical support, and so on.
- ☐ Meeting management ground rules and plan for continual improvement
- ☐ Metrics and measurement process
  - ▫ Monitor performance in all functions such as sales, marketing, manufacturing, customer service, technical service and support, and finance
  - ▫ Tracking of all relevant measure: penetration of targets, total customer experience (all interactions or missed interactions with company), units, revenue, Average Selling Price (ASP), customer feedback, complaints, returned product, and response to customer and continual customer feedback
  - ▫ Monitor revenue, gross profit, and EBIT projections compared with monthly results
- ☐ Tracking (units, sales, ASP, profitability by customer, satisfaction), reporting, communication plan
- ☐ Continual improvement: addressing urgent issues, collecting and reporting success stories, and effective problem identification and resolution in regular (weekly, monthly, quarterly, biannual, and/or annual meetings)

Product

- ☐ Product competitive advantages and pricing
  - ▫ Ensure that product meets product requirements: *required* (must occur or product is not introduced) and *desired* (valuable features that provide advantages; however, they will not be included if they have significant negative impact on quality, cost, or timing). *Required* features are tested in the quality process prior to shipping and were satisfactorily achieved in a *pilot* of selected customers

- Manufacturing and distribution challenged to optimally deliver on quality, cost, and volume, and working with the product introduction team on trade-offs.
- Document product fit with other company products (addressing potential cannibalization and how to upsell and cross-sell in the context of other products)
- Fulfill all regulatory requirements, such as documentation for filing and quality system

Pricing

- ☐ Pricing approaches and decisions
  - Reimbursement documented: who pays what, when, and how for the product and therapy is documented and clear
  - value-based, competitive positioning and response, niche or mass market, progression over next five years
  - Pricing developed in the context of delivered value to the customer, market, and competitive conditions
  - Pricing offers: purchase, rent, lease, shared risk and reward, predictable pricing, disposable-only options
  - Contract templates for most common situations

Promotion

- ☐ Go to market strategy
  - Market segments are defined and in priority order. High-value targets are listed in priority order with business impact documented (sales, profit, strategic value)
  - High-value customers mapped by name on the innovation curve—with focus on innovators and early adopters
  - Documented decision process for selling to the highest-value targets: who is the *fox* (can veto or push through the sale), decision makers, and influencers
  - Process is defined and plan is documented to create raving fans

- ☐ Communication with customers
  - ☐ Messaging and value propositions including monetized benefits are created for clinical and economic buyers at strategic, managerial, and operational levels
  - ☐ Process and analysis of the *voice of the customer* : systematic input from target segment on awareness, brand, messages, pricing, behavior preferences, benchmarking study, or conclusions (see an example in Appendix 1)
- ☐ Information gathering system: Continual conversations with informed people–customers, prospects, advisors, sales peoples, customer service research and development, competitors, technical service via conferences, meetings, websites, chat rooms, blogs, journals, press releases, surveys (web, phone, or face to face), phone, and e-mail.
  - ☐ Analysis of business potential: revenue, gross profit, cannibalization, competitive responses, or advances
  - ☐ Analysis of unmet needs: feature, benefits, or value
  - ☐ Competitive advantage analysis: benefits or value compared to current and future alternatives
- ☐ Develop trusted advisors from leading institutions that direct creation of more raving fans:
  - ☐ Collaborate on product development, messages for improved clinical outcomes and lower total costs (source *Nephrology News and Issues* article), pricing, competitive positioning, future needs
  - ☐ The product introduction plan is first implemented for and critiqued by this group
  - ☐ Proof statements: well-designed studies, observational studies, case studies, registry or collection of data, publications, presentations, posters, abstracts, white papers, editorials, testimonials
  - ☐ Reference center preparation process: e-mail, phone, visits to site, visits of experts from this site to others
  - ☐ Ensure sufficient usage of the product to validate product quality and gain meaningful input to all major decisions

- ☐ Fundamental selling approaches in place
  - ☐ Description of the customer buying process
  - ☐ Plans for prospecting, precall planning, and effective conversations with customers
  - ☐ Win–win negotiating and objection handling
  - ☐ Closing the sale and creating raving fans
  - ☐ Sales management plans for
    - ☐ Territory and time management and ethics
    - ☐ Declaration of the company's key professional selling concepts
    - ☐ Sales representative selection and recruiting
    - ☐ Maximizing performance: expectations, motivation, compensation, incentives, and evaluation
    - ☐ Sales training with accelerated learning principles and techniques
- ☐ Sales support tools
  - ☐ Questions to lead customers to your competitive advantages
  - ☐ Messages for feature, benefit, and value that makes customers say "WOW!, how did they do that." For competitive advantages, messages for 20 seconds, 2 minutes, and 20 minutes
  - ☐ Messages for pricing rationale, customers to trap or inoculate competitive responses, responding to objections
  - ☐ Proof statement development: implement plan for well-designed studies, observational studies, case studies, registry or collection of data, publications, presentations, posters, abstracts, white papers, editorials, testimonials
  - ☐ Tools that address customer needs, including promotional materials, proof statements, value calculator, animation, user videos.
  - ☐ Matrix that matches tools by company objectives such as (1) get customers, (2) keep customers, and (3) grow customers. Matrix that matches customer's needs to company tools.

- ☐ Communications strategy to customers: Direct from CEO, VP, or sales to targets; e-mail; webinar; podcasts; web; industry events (annual meetings); journals; web, and so on.
- ☐ Systematic sales training using accelerated learning, online courses, tests, coaching and video feedback, certification tests, and ongoing sales process (stages) and improvement
- ☐ Reward and recognition: motivational incentive plan—with input from those who will administer and get the commission; motivational recognition plan including recognition events for monthly, quarterly, and annual results, as well as for significant events.
- ☐ Pipeline management:
  - ☐ Target institutions: fox, decision makers, influencers, advocates, or foes; alliance with national accounts
  - ☐ Value selling: selling process—qualify and move from 50 percent to close, clear, and transparent reporting
  - ☐ Try, buy, repeat, and grow
  - ☐ Message and tool creation as objections are raised
- ☐ Raving fan development: Define *raving fan* or *ideal customer* with action plans on how to help the customer achieve this level of satisfaction

Appendixes

Appendix 1

*Sample Benchmarking Study Outline: Syndicated Market
Research Company*

1. Study overview and design
2. Familiarity with *Syndicated Report* Providers
3. *Reports* Relied Upon Most
4. Main Competitors
5. Ratings of Company and Main Competitors
6. Advantages and Disadvantages of Company
7. Advantages and Disadvantages of Competitors
8. Strong Statements Describing Company Studied and its Products
9. Strong Statements Describing Competition
10. Process of Searching, Selecting and Purchasing Reports
11. Estimates for Generating DR Information In-house
12. Awareness and Use of Decision Resources Products and Services
13. Communications about New Reports and Improvements. Awareness
14. Recommendations to Improve Usage
15. Purposes for Which DR Products are Used
16. Job Support and Utility Provided by Decision Resources Products
17. Needs Not Met By DR and its Products
18. Needs and Concerns which DR could Address
19. Ideas for Better Partnering with Companies
20. Suggestions for Improvements
21. Interest Level in Proposed New Services

Appendix 2

Sample Aviation Checklist*

Introduction

Aviation is very procedural. Every action you will undertake in the aircraft will have a checklist tied to it somewhere. Many of the checklists are simple and can be memorized, but this is not always a good practice. Memories can be faulty, and in aviation, a faulty memory can be a death sentence. Use your checklists.

Here is an example of a preflight checklist for a 1967 Cessna 150:

1. Remove Control Locks and Tie down Ropes
2. Master—On
3. Flaps—Down
4. Fuel Gauge—Check
5. Master—Off
6. Ignition (MAGS)—Off
7. Throttle—Closed (Pulled Out)
8. Mixture—Lean (Pulled Out)
9. Sample Fuel (Check for Water and Sediment)—Left Wing
10. Inspect Left Side of Fuselage for Damage
11. Inspect Leading Edge of Horizontal and Vertical Stabilizer for Damage
12. Inspect Skin on Tail Surfaces for Damage
13. Check Stabilizers, Elevator, and Rudder for excessive travel
14. Check that Hinge Bolts are fastened and Cotter Pins are in Place on Tail Surfaces
15. Inspect Right Side of Fuselage for Damage
16. Drain Fuel (Check for Water and Sediment)—Right Wing
17. Check Flaps for excessive travel, bolts are fastened, and Control Rod is attached and is not bent

---

* http://www.pilotfriend.com/flightplanning/flight%20planning/vfr_checklist.htm

18. Check Ailerons for excessive travel, hinges are attached and not Cracked, Cotter Pins are attached to hinge ends

19. Remove all Ice Formation from Aileron

20. Check that Lead Weights are attached to Aileron

21. Shake Right Wing Up and Down—Check for tightness and unusual Sounds

22. Check Wing Struts—Check for tightness and unusual sounds

23. Inspect Right Wing for Damage—Check for Wrinkles

24. Inspect Main Landing Gear for Damage

25. Inspect Main Landing Gear Tire for proper inflation, cuts, condition of tread, or foreign objects (screws or nails in tire)

26. Inspect Brake Pads for wear

27. Inspect Brake Line for leaks

28. Check that Wheel is fastened to Landing Gear (Cotter Pin is in Place)

29. Check Oil Level (4½ Quarts Minimum to Six Quarts Maximum)

30. Check Oil Breather for blockage

31. Drain Fuel from Fuel Strainer

32. Check Inside the Cowling (Nose of Aircraft) for loose Wiring, Oil Leaks, Fuel Leaks, All Engine Accessories are installed and installed correctly

33. Check that Cowling is fastened correctly—All Screws are attached

34. Check Propeller and Spinner—Check for Damage and Security

35. Check Engine Baffle—Check for Damage and Security

36. Check Engine Baffle Seals—Check for Damage and Security

37. Check Engine Exhaust Pipes—Check for Damage and Security

38. Check Carburetor Air Filter—Clean

39. Inspect Nose Gear for Damage and Proper Inflation (two inch spread on Nose Strut)

40. Inspect Nose Gear Shimmy Dampener for Damage

41. Check that all Bolts and Nuts are attached to nose fork assembly

42. Inspect Nose Gear Tire for proper inflation, cuts, condition of Tread, or foreign objects (screws or nails in tire)

43. Check that Wheel is fastened to Nose Gear—Bolt and Nut Attached

44. Check Condition of Steering Rod Boots
45. Check Static Port for Damage and Obstructions
46. Check Radio Cooling Vent for Damage and Obstructions
47. Check Pitot Tube for Damage and Obstructions
48. Check Fuel Overflow Tube for Damage and Obstructions
49. Check Stall Warning Port for Damage and Obstructions
50. Check Wing Struts—Check for tightness and unusual sounds
51. Inspect Left Wing for Damage—Check for Wrinkles
52. Shake Left Wing Up and Down—Check for tightness and unusual sounds
53. Check Ailerons for excessive travel, hinges are attached and not cracked, Cotter Pins are attached to hinge ends, Control Rod attached
54. Remove All Ice Formation from Aileron
55. Check that Lead Weights are attached to Aileron
56. Check Flaps for excessive travel, bolts are fastened, and Control Rod is attached and is not bent
57. Inspect Main Landing Gear for Damage
58. Inspect Main Landing Gear Tire for Proper inflation, cuts, condition of tread, or foreign objects (screws or nails in tire)
59. Inspect Brake Pads for wear
60. Inspect Brake Line for leaks
61. Check that Wheel is fastened to Landing Gear (Cotter Pin is in place)
62. Check Left Fuel Tank
63. Check Right Fuel Tank
64. Check Top of Wings for Damage
65. Remove all Ice Formation from the Top and Bottom of All Surfaces
66. Check Navigation Lights, Landing Lights, Strobe Lights, Pulse Light System, and the Beacon for Damage and Proper Illumination
67. Check Antennas for Damage
68. Remove all Debris under Propeller (rocks etc.)
69. Fold up Step Ladder and put it in the bed of the truck

Appendix 3

Operationally excellent firms maintain a strong competitive advantage by maintaining exceptional efficiency, thus enabling the firm to provide reliable service to the customer at a significantly lower cost than those of less well-organized and well-run competitors. The emphasis here is mostly on low cost, subject to reliable performance, and less value is put on customizing the offering for the specific customer. Wal-Mart is an example of this discipline. Elaborate logistical designs allow goods to be moved at the lowest cost, with extensive systems predicting when specific quantities of supplies will be needed.

Customer intimate firms excel in serving the specific needs of the individual customer well. There is less emphasis on efficiency, which is sacrificed for providing more precisely what is wanted by the customer. Reliability is also stressed. Nordstrom's and IBM are examples of this discipline.

Technologically excellent firms, which produce the most advanced products currently available with the latest technology, constantly maintaining leadership in innovation. These firms, because they work with costly technology that need constant refinement, cannot be as efficient as the operationally excellent firms and also cannot often adapt their products to the needs of the individual customer. Intel is an example of this discipline (Hogan and Lucke 2004; Treacy and Wiersema 1993).

Appendix 4

Be Your Own Brand

We all have a brand, whether we like it or know it. A personal brand is simply a message, a thought. It is what other people think of when they think of you. It is the sum total of what people know about you. Every time you interact with another person, you are influencing your brand. What is your brand? Do you talk about big ideas? Are you clear and concise? Are you interesting? Do people pay attention to you?

People have a feeling about others as soon as they meet them. They continue to shape that feeling with subsequent interactions. When another person sees you, they register a positive, neutral or negative feeling. It is in your power to influence that feeling and make it positive every time.

A powerful person's brand

- Is instantly recognizable
- Stands for something of value
- Builds trust
- Generates positive word of mouth
- Gives a competitive advantage
- Creates career opportunity
- Results in professional and financial success

Many people have the tools to create a strong personal brand. How do you create a buzz about yourself? One way is to start speaking in formal and informal settings. Speaking inside and outside your company positions you as an expert for several reasons:

- Many of your colleagues or competitors don't do it.
- People assume that if you are speaking on a topic you are an expert.
- Other people promote your talk.
- You are center stage, which automatically gives you credibility.
- If you give a valuable talk, then people remember you.
- If they remember you, then you become top of mind and you are the one they think of when they refer someone for new business, promotions, other speaking engagements, and so on.

Wherever you are in your career, you can start sending strong, positive signals that will create buzz for you. You have the power, and need, to create your own personal brand. If not you, then who? If not now, then when? The more people you help through work and by sharing your insights, the more value you bring to others. This can create a virtuous cycle of you giving and receiving value to more and more people (Bates 2006, 27).

Appendix 5

master salesmanship

The newsletter for professional salespeople

VOL. 12 ISSUE 21
OCTOBER 8, 1990

Do questions really make the sale?

by Jack Falvey
President, Intermark

Is the presentation the most important part of the sale? Is the close? Are good questions the common element in all sales, in all industries? Are closing questions used by sales professionals at all levels? Are informational questions necessary on every call, no matter how well you may know your prospect? Are people offended by directional questions that tend to move the selling process along (i.e.,) "Where do we go from here?" "Would a trial order be appropriate?" "Can we set up a meeting (test) (pilot program)?"

Which questions work best for you with your accounts? What are some of your best closing questions? What do you really know about your customers? Did they go to college? Where? When? What did they study? Are they married? How many times? Do they have children? How many? What are they doing? Do they drink? At lunch? What do they drink? Do they smoke? What brand? Are they involved in civic activities? What do they like to talk about? Where did they go on vacation last year? Where are they going this year? When? For how long?

What are they most proud of in business? Where have they worked? Lived? What do they hope to accomplish in their present assignment? What do they think their next job will be? When? Who is their boss? When are they given performance and/or salary reviews? What are they reviewed upon? What are their short-term goals? Long-term? What are their boss's goals? What do they consider to be the strength of the organization? What do they think their own strength is? How are new products or services evaluated? Is there a contract period? Who has the business now? How did they get it? Why did they get it? Is price a big issue? Is it the most important issue? What would cause a change in vendors? Who are the key decision makers? What do they look for? Can you call on them? Are trials appropriate? Can you do a study or a survey? What would be the ideal in your product or service category?

What do you like best about your current system? (prospect's) What do you like least? If you were me, how would you proceed? What do you view as my company's strengths? What are the quality levels you are willing to pay for? How important are in-house inventory levels? How important is training? How important is service? What is the ideal shipping frequency? Are there new products in the works? What are the lead times? How can I get involved? Are there other locations I should know about? How im-

Organizing your sales presentation

There are several ways to organize your sales presentation. You may have one standard approach or use different methods to suit each individual customer. The important thing is to be organized so as not to confuse the prospect. Here are some approaches that have worked well for many salespeople.

1. Logical approach. Before you make your presentation, find out what your prospect's needs are. Then tailor your pitch around his or her way of thinking. You must gradually lead the prospect from his or her mode of thinking to yours. The key points to stress are economy, efficiency and uniformity.

2. Chronological approach. Give your prospect a history of your product, including development, testing, construction, applications, advantages and unique features. By the end of your presentation, your prospect should know exactly what your product can do for him or her.

3. Emotional approach. This approach works best for products that have an educational or protective value. Your presentation should begin with specific facts and descriptions and end with an appeal to the emotion.

portant are transportation costs? Are government contracts involved? Are there trade associations you belong to? Should I join? What are the professional journals you subscribe to? What business books do you read? What's the best book on the business?

Can we get down to business? What will it take to get an order? Do you have a purchase number you can give me? Is it a deal? Can we begin? What's next? Is a trial appropriate? How about a four-month test? Can we ship immediately? How soon can we begin? Does someone else have to approve this? Will these quantities work? Do you think you will need back-up inventory? When can we start saving all this excess cost?

Can we schedule your people for training? Can you attend an executive briefing? Can I bring our president to visit? Will this pilot program expand overseas in ninety days?

Do we have any foreign exchange problems to work out? Can you get me a letter of credit? No credit difficulties? On the initial order, can we have fifty percent up front?

Can you fax the instructions to your purchasing people? Do you want me to hand carry the paperwork? Can I check to see if we have sufficient capacity? Can you visit a beta site on next Thursday or Friday? Is there anyone else that should make the trip? You don't mind a short helicopter ride, do you?

Can you tell me why you decided against us? Why would you say that? (smile) What is my best shot to get back the account? Can you continue to use us at least as a second source? Is there a small piece of secondary business we can have just so I'm not closed out? What would it take to get back in? How about running in tandem for awhile just so the changeover will be sure to work? Is there any way I can help your new supplier?

What did we do on the last sale that most impressed you? What are our strengths? What are my strengths (if any)? What do you look for in a vendor relationship? What do you look for in a vendor sales rep? Who was the best sales rep you ever had call on you? Who was the worst? Do you have time for lunch? When is the best time for me to call back? What else can I do for you?

Hasn't this been a different article? You already know the importance of using questions to get needed information and to help prospects make decisions that move the sale to a successful close. So I just packed in a lot of examples of questions that have worked for me and other salespeople to win and keep more customers. Jot down those you think you might use as you read them again. Add your own successful questions to the list and review them all from time to time until they become automatic when the right situation arises.

Why not do it? Why not do it NOW?

Jack Falvey is a popular speaker for conventions and sales meetings, and a consultant in sales and management. He is a columnist and writer for Wall Street Journal, Sales & Marketing Management, and other publications. He is the author of books and producer of training films. His most recent book is The Absolute Very Best of Jack Falvey on Sales Management, a collection of his key articles in leading publications. Contact: Intermark, 22 Cortland Drive, Londonderry, NH 03053, or call 1-800-241-7308.

References

American Salesman. 2006. "Consultative Selling Now Seen as Biggest Challenge." September, p. 29.

Baron, N. 2010. "The Magic Question that Accelerates Sales." *Fast Company*, April 7. http://www.fastcompany.com/1608731/magic-question-accelerates-sales

Bates, S. 2006. "Is There Buzz About You? The Power of Building a Personal Brand." *American Salesman*, October, p. 27.

Decker, B. 2008. *You've Got to Be Believed to Be Heard*. New York: St. Martin's Press.

Dixon, M., and B. Adamson. 2011. "Selling Is Not About Relationships." https://hbr.org/2011/09/selling-is-not-about-relatio

Falvey, J. 2014. "Selling Tips of the Day." www.makingthenumbers.com

Gawande, A. 2010. *The Checklist Manifesto: How to Get Things Right*. New York: Metropolitan Books.

Gladwell, M. 2002. *The Tipping Point*. Boston, MA: Back Bay Books.

Graham, J.R. 2008. "The Seven Strategies of the Highly Effective Salesperson." *American Salesman*, July, p. 12.

Hogan, J.E., and T. Lucke. September 14, 2004. "How to Avoid New Product Pricing Traps." http://www.marketingprofs.com/4/lucke1.asp

Johnston, M., and G. Marshall. 2009. *Relationship Selling*. 3rd ed. Boston, MA: McGraw-Hill/Irwin.

Kanzer, R., and J. Westman. 2002. "Powerful Meetings." http://www.robkanzer.com/news/effectivemeetings.htm

Kennedy, K.N., F.G. Lassk, and J.R. Goolsby. 2002. "Customer Mind-Set of Employees Throughout the Organization." *Journal of the Academy of Marketing Science* 30, no. 2, pp. 159–71.

Kotler, P. 1999. *Kotler on Marketing: How to Create, Win and Dominate Markets*. New York: Free Press.

Lehman, D.R., and K.E. Jocz, eds. 1997. *Reflections on the Futures of Marketing*. Cambridge, MA: Marketing Science Institute.

Manktelow, J., and A. Carlson. n.d. "Active Listening." http://www.mindtools.com/CommSkll/ActiveListening.htm

Marshall, G.W., D.J. Goebel, and W.C. Moncrief. March 2003. "Hiring for Success at the Buyer-Seller Interface." *Journal of Business Research* 56, no. 4, pp. 247–55.

Mrazek, D. December 2007. "How to Evolve Beyond Networking into the R-Zone." *American Salesman* 52, no. 12, p. 27.

Peppers, D., and M. Rogers. January 2011. *Customer Relationship Management: A Strategic Framework.* New York, NY: Wiley.

Pink, D. 2013. *To Sell Is Human.* New York: Riverhead Trade.

Rackham, N., and J. DeVincentis. 1999. *Rethinking the Sales Force: Redefining Selling to Create and Capture Customer Value.* New York: McGraw-Hill.

Richmond, K. 2010. The Power of Selling. Open Textbook library. http://open. umn.edu/opentextbooks/BookDetail.aspx?bookId=42

Rogers, E.M. 2003. *Diffusion of Innovations.* New York: Free Press.

Thousand, J., and R. Villa. 1995. "Managing Complex Change Toward Inclusive Schooling." *In* Creating an Inclusive School, eds. R.A. Villa and J.S. Thousand, 51–79. Alexandria, VA: Association for Supervision and Curriculum Development.

Treacy, M., and F. Wiersema. 1993. *The Discipline of Market Leaders.*

Wikipedia. 2014. Robert Cialdini. http://en.wikipedia.org/wiki/Robert_Cialdini

Ziglar, Z. 2003. *Selling 101: What Every Successful Sales Professional Needs to Know.* Nashville, TN: Thomas Nelson.

Index

Adamson, Brent, 42
Advertising, 5
  marketing metrics and, 10
  promotion plan and, 26, 34
Assessment
  customer development, 81–82
  market, 25
Attitude, winning, 28–29
Authority, 57
Awareness, in sales process, 62

Behaviors at meeting, 70
Best practices, 7, 23, 55, 76, 86,
    119–120
Beyond the product, 34
Boyle, Steven L., 106
Brand names, 4
Brand promise, 94–95
Branding, 131–132
*Breakthrough Ideas for Today's Business
    Agenda* (Cialdini), 56
Building relationships by salesperson,
    71–74
Buyers, 62
Buying signals, 60

CEO
  context for, 3
  marketing function, 15
  Marketing Pyramid and, 1–3
  new product launch, 1–5
  overriding goal of, 1–2
  worldview, 2
Challengers, salesperson as, 43
Checklist
  leadership and management,
      16–22, 121–122
  new product launch, vii–viii,
      119–126
  pricing, 123
  product, 122–123

promotion, 123–126
  sample Aviation, 128–130
Churchill, Winston, 23
Cialdini, Robert B., 56–57
Clayton Act, 103
Closing techniques, 59–60
Code of conduct, 104
Code of Ethics for salespeople, 106
Collusion, as unlawful business
    activity, 103
Commitment and consistency, 56–57
Competitor defamation, 103
Competitor obstruction, 103
Connectors, 38
Consultative selling, 45
Consulting group, 99–100
Context, 38–39
Controller, 62
CRM. *See* customer relationship
    management
Cross functional leadership, 10
Cross-fertilization, 38
Customer
  promise to, 96–97
  voice of the, 97–99
Customer buying process, 60–62
Customer concerns, 76
  compensating for deficiencies as, 78
  customer's feelings as, 78–79
  direct denial as, 77
  early pricing as, 79–80
  indirect denial as, 78
  into reason for action, 79
  questioning as, 77
  third party endorsements as, 79
  trial offer as, 80
Customer development, 12, 81–82
Customer input-observation,
    101–102
Customer relationship management
    (CRM), 109–111

Customer strategic planning group, 100

Customers, helping, 76

Decision making, 5
    HPWT and, 6
Dell Computer, 104
Design, product, 4
Direct professional selling. *See* professional selling
Direct Selling Association, 106
Directional questions, 52
DiSC approach, 53
Dixon, Mathew, 42
Dorn, Randy, 67–68

Eades, Keith, 46
Effectiveness
    HPWT and, 7
    team leadership, 7
Efficiency, HPWT and, 7
Employee skills and capabilities, 5
Empowerment of employees, 5
Enterprise selling, 45
Environment/historical moment, 38
Ethical behaviors, 104–107
Ethical standards of sales person, 104–106

Farley, John, 1, 15
Features, product, 4
Filters, 62
Financial assessment, 36
Follow-up skills, 52
Full conversion strategy, 115–116

Gatekeepers, 62
George, David Lloyd, 85
Gide, Andre, 119
Gladwell, Malcolm, 38
Go-to-market plan, 117

Hard workers, salesperson as, 42
Harkins, Phil, 19

Helping customers, 76
High-performance work teams (HPWT)
    characteristics of
        developing and implementing plans, 6
        development opportunities for team members, 7
        effective team leadership, 7
        informational meetings, 6
        managing conflicts, 6
        positive relationships among members, 6
        productive meetings, 6
        role for team members, 6–7
    overview of, 5
    problem-solving and decision-making by, 6
High-value targets, 35–37
Hot button selling, 58

Implication questions, 73
Influencers, 62
Initiators, 61
Instructions, survey and, 9
Interest, in sales process, 62
International Code of Ethics for Sales and Marketing, 107–109

Johnson, David W., 119

Keith, Robert, 1
Keller, Helen, 55, 119

Leadership and management, 16–22
    checklist, 121–122
Legal/ethical considerations for sales person, 102–107
Lifetime value, 35–36
Listening, active, 49–51
Listening skills, 47–53
Listening/validating customer concerns, 76
Lombardi, Vincent T., 85
Lone wolves, salesperson as, 43

Magic Questions for sales, 93–94
Market assessment, 25
Market intelligence, 4
Market knowledge, 4, 9
Market place, 45–46, 116–117
Market segments, 35–37
Marketing
   function, 15
   management, 9
   metrics, 10
   mix, 4, 33–54
   plan, 4, 100
   process, 15–16
   and sales tools, 12–13
   strategies, 9–10
   team, 4–5
Marketing Diagnostic tool
   four "4Ps"
      place or distribution, 13–14, 16
      pricing, 13, 16
      product enhancements, 9–10, 16
      promotion, 11–13, 16
   objectives, 8
   process description, 8
   summary, 14
   survey and instructions, 9
   value of, 8–9
Marketing distribution. *See* Market
      place
Marketing 4P's
   framework, 33–54, 34
   place (distribution), 13–14, 16
   pricing, 13, 16
   product, 10, 16
   promotion, 11–13, 16
Marketing Pyramid, 1–3
Materials, marketing, 5
Maugham, W. Somerset, 85
Mavens, 38
Meetings, 18–22, 70
Message delivery, 11
Messages, 11
Messaging, 55–57, 92–93
Metrics, 29–31
Myers-Briggs approach, 53

Need-payoff questions, 73
Negotiation, win-win situation in,
      74–76
Networking, 65–66
New product and product upgrade
      pipeline, 10
New product launch
   buying process, 60–62
   CEO and, 1–5
   checklist, 119–126
   closing technique, 59–60
   conditions for
      resources to fund required
         programs, 26–27
      SMART goals, 24
      strategies, 24–26
      team composition, 27
      three-step change model, 27–28
      vision, 23–24
      winning attitude, 28–29
   context of, 1–5
   creating raving fans, 81–82
   customer concerns, 76–80
   messaging, 55–57
   metrics, 29–31
   objection handling, 58–59
   pretenders and, vii
   professional selling and, 64–74
   relationship selling, description of,
      57–58
   team leadership approach for,
      23–31
   win-win negotiations, 74–76
Niche strategy, 115

Objection handling, 58–59, 77–80
One-minute rule in meetings, 20

Packaging, 4
Parks, Gordon, 119
Persuasion equation, 28
Pink, Daniel, 57–58
Place (distribution), 5, 13–14, 16,
      116–117
postmeeting actions, 70

Premeeting planning, 70
Presentations, sales, 68–69
Price discrimination, as unlawful
        business activity, 103
Pricing
    checklist, 123
    product, 112–116
    strategies, 4, 13, 16
Problem questions, 73
Problem solving, 5
    HPWT and, 6
Process description, 8
Product
    checklist, 122–123
    decisions about, 33
    distribution channels, 116–117
    enhancement, 9–10, 16, 35
    introduction team, 30–31
    quality, 4
    names, 34
Professional selling, 39, 87–88
    fundamentals of, 64–66
Profiling styles of salesperson, 53
Promise to customer, 96–97
Promotion, 4–5, 11–13, 16
    checklist, 123–126
    message delivery, 11
    plan, 111
    segmentation and targeting, 11
Proof development, 12
*Powerful Conversations: How High
        Impact Leaders Communicate*
        (Harkins), 19

Questioning, 47–53
Questions
    directional, 51, 52
    implication, 73
    informational, 51, 52
    need-payoff, 73
    problem, 73
    professional selling fundamental,
        64–65
    situation, 73

Raving fans, 81–82
Reactive problem solvers, salesperson
        as, 43

Reciprocity, 56
Relationship builders, salesperson as, 42
Relationship selling, 57–58
    versus transactional selling, 44
Resources to fund required programs,
        26–27
Rogers adoption curve, 33
Restraint of trade, as unlawful
        business activity, 103
Robinson-Patman Act, 103

Sale and Marketing Executives
        International (SMEI), 107
Sales
    Magic Questions for, 93–94
    sales training, 13
Sales force composition, 4–5
Sales management lesson, 51–52,
        63–64
Sales objectives, 67
Salespersons, 38
    building relationships by, 71–74
    as challengers, 43
    Code of Ethics for, 106
    conversation with customers by,
        66–71
    ethical standards of, 104–107
    follow-up skills of, 52
    as hard workers, 43
    legal and ethical considerations for,
        102–107
    listening and questioning skills of,
        47–53
    as lone wolves, 43
    objection handling by, 77–80
    profiles of, 42–44
    profiling styles of, 53
    as reactive problem solvers, 43
    as relationship builders, 42
    spending time by, 88–89
    success factors for, 83
    tenacity of, 53–54
    territory and time management, 89
    underpromise and overdeliver by,
        52–53
    unlawful business activities by, 103
Sales presentations, 68–69
Sales process, 62

Sales training, 85–87
Sample Aviation checklist, 128–130
Scarcity, 57
Scientific advisory board, 101
Screeners, 62
Segmentation and targeting, 4, 11
Selling
    consultative, 44–45
    enterprise, 45
    hot button, 58
    professional, 64–66, 87–88
    relationship, 44, 57–58
    solution, 46
    transactional, 44
Senior management, 16–17
Sherman Antitrust Act, 103
Situation questions, 73
Size, product, 4
Social proof, 57
Solution selling, 46
SMART (specific, measurable,
        actionable, realistic, time
        bound), 23
SMART goals, 24
SMEI. See Sale and Marketing
        Executives International
SPIN approach, 73
Stakeholders, 8–9
Standard Marketing 4Ps Fundamental
        Diagnostic Survey, 8–9
Stickiness, 38
Strategies, market, 24–26
Strode, Muriel, 55
Survey, Marketing Diagnostic, 8, 9
SWOT (strengths, weaknesses,
        opportunities, threats), 25
Syndicated Market Research
        Company, 127

Team behavior, sample, 17–18
Team composition, 27
Team leader, 16–17
Teammates, 16–17
Territory and time management, 89
Thought leader roll-out plan, 37–38
Three-step change model, 27–28
Time management, 89
Tipping point, 33, 38
    connectors, mavens and salesmen,
        38
    context, 38–39
    stickiness, 38
Training, sales. See Sales training
Transactional selling versus
        relationship selling, 44

UCC. See Uniform Commercial Code
        (UCC)
Ultrabag 1992, 114–115
Uniform Commercial Code (UCC),
        102
Unique quality, 38
Unlawful business activities, 103
Users, product, 62

Value of Diagnostic Survey, 8–9
Value proposition, 25, 40–41, 68,
        90–92
Varieties, product, 4
Vision, 23–24
Voice of the customer, 97–99

Winning attitude, 28–29
Win-win negotiations, 74–76

CPSIA information can be obtained at www.ICGtesting.com
Printed in the USA
BVOW05s0850121115

426471BV00005B/35/P